MAVERICK REAL ESTATE INVESTING

MAVERICK REAL ESTATE INVESTING

The Art of Buying and Selling
Properties Like Trump, Zell,
Simon, and the World's Greatest
Land Owners

STEVE BERGSMAN

WILEY

John Wiley & Sons, Inc.

Published by John Wiley & Sons, Inc., Hoboken, New Jersey.
Published simultaneously in Canada.

For general information on our other products and services, or technical support, please contact our Customer Care Department within the United States at 800-762-2974, outside the United States at 317-572-3993 or fax 317-572-4002.

Wiley also publishes its books in a variety of electronic formats. Some content that appears in print may not be available in electronic books.

For more information about Wiley products, visit our web site at www.wiley.com.
Library of Congress Cataloging-in-Publication Data:

Bergsman, Steve.
    Maverick real estate investing : the art of buying and selling properties like Trump, Zell, Simon, and the world's greatest land owners / Steve Bergsman.
        p. cm.
Includes index.
ISBN 0-471-46879-7 (CLOTH)
1. Real estate investment. I. Title.
HD1382.5.B467 2004
332.63'24—dc22   2003020244
Printed in the United States of America

10 9 8 7 6 5 4 3 2

Contents

Introduction

Long before I began writing about real estate, once—and only once—I tried my hand at property investing. Three associates and I formed a limited partnership and began buying small homes to rent. We got as deep into our scheme as you can with a portfolio of two houses when it quickly became apparent that our venture was an absolute disaster. Looking back more than a decade later, it is clear that our partnership failed because we violated almost every tenet of successful real estate investing.

To begin with, we didn't even get that legendary doggerel about real estate—"location, location, location"—right. While one house was in a good neighborhood, the other was in a marginal area where it was difficult to attract reliable, nondestructive tenants.

The first house sat on a quiet cul-de-sac in Tempe, Arizona, a suburban community southeast of Phoenix. There was nothing fancy about the house. It sported three bedrooms, a single-car garage, and was in appealing condition. The tenants were a nice family that included two small children. As far as we could tell, they were respectful of the property. It seemed like we couldn't go wrong on this one.

We found the second home in Mesa, Arizona, one of the fastest-growing communities in the country during the 1980s and 1990s. Unfortunately, the neighborhood we chose was in transition—and going the wrong way.

The Mesa house boasted a swimming pool, which we thought would be an attraction—and it was. But our tenants, who were friends of friends, had never lived in a house with a swimming pool before and proceeded to turn the clear blue waters a swampy green. Eventually, a pool service had to be brought in to rescue the situation.

The friends of friends apparently didn't know much about electric ranges, either, because they managed to blow out that appliance in just two weeks.

The Mesa house was rented in the spring, just before the onset of the very hot summer months, which meant the yard, including lawn and shrubbery, had to be regularly watered and maintained. By the time we got the friends of friends—who by now had lost their jobs—out of the house, the once green yard had been returned to desert dust. Barely one leafy thing survived.

And those were just the *fun* times during our days as landlords!

Since we could afford only a small amount for our down payments, the mortgages were higher than the cash flow that came in from the individual leases. Obviously, we didn't understand the ramifications of what this would mean to our bottom line.

On top of that, none of us was handy with repairs. As a result, the properties were expensive to keep up and manage. To make matters worse, we bought the homes just as the local housing market was going into a downturn, so the value of the properties almost immediately headed south.

Perhaps the worst ignominy we suffered was that our investment group included a residential real estate broker, who traded his expertise for a position in the partnership—with no initial cash investment required. Our so-called expert was supposed to take care of the books. Instead, he farmed out that chore to his live-in girl-friend, who proceeded to steal the partnership's meager funds. Our "expert" ultimately made up for the losses, but he had to be forced out. When he went, we lost our only knowledgeable partner. We eventually wound up selling both homes at a loss.

I bring up this sad story to illustrate that there are so many ways a real estate investment can go bad, especially if you don't know what you're doing.

It is often said that real estate is about the only sure investment a person can make. How wrong that is! Real estate appears to be a sure thing to the uninformed, but it more regularly proves to be fool's gold.

There are, however, some real estate investors who seem to con-tinually win big. They have built substantial fortunes through astute deal making and visionary thinking, while making sure their vast property empires are managed to maximum effect. These rare indi-viduals are the true Mavericks of real estate investing.

Some—such as Donald Trump, Sam Zell, Eli Broad, Paul Reich-mann, Samuel LeFrak, and Melvin Simon—are well known. Others—including Walter Shorenstein, Hamid Moghadam, Gerald Hines, John Kukral, and Stuart Hornery—keep a much lower pro-file, yet have enjoyed similar success.

What sets these Mavericks apart from everyone else? Quite sim-ply, they follow the 12 golden rules of real estate investing, all of which we will explore in this book. Among their rules: Make a good deal; understand cycles; use other people's money; establish cash flow targets; be in alignment; find a nearly perfect location; benefit from someone else's disasters; make safe gambles; hire savvy man-agers; get good legal and tax counsel; overcome negative responses; and sell to your advantage.

Each chapter in *Maverick Real Estate Investing* examines one of these rules and provides specific examples of how they have success-fully been applied over the years by the Mavericks themselves. The first part of each chapter looks at the theories behind the rule, and the second half provides a brief biography of the colorful career of the Maverick or Mavericks who best demonstrate this axiom in action. That way you can see how they began and were able to expand their respective companies into the powerhouses they are today.

Granted, not all of the Mavericks are foolproof. Some have stum-bled badly along the way. For example, in the 1980s the Reichmann brothers of Canada formed Olympia & York Development—at the time the biggest and most successful global real estate company—only to see it fall into bankruptcy as the cycle turned against it and debt mounted too fast for the firm to be saved. Donald Trump, too, almost lost his entire empire during the crushing real estate depres-sion of the late 1980s and early 1990s.

As astute and seasoned investors, both the Reichmanns and Trump were able to resurrect their businesses, albeit in smaller forms, by the late 1990s. They continue to thrive today.

The featured Mavericks run the gamut in terms of what kind of real estate they invest in. Some specialize in commercial properties, while others focus on the residential side of the business. A few are even involved in raising big pots of capital to fund a variety of dif-ferent investments that are then run by other managers.

While most of the Mavericks hail from the United States, some are based in other parts of the world. The Reichmanns live in Canada. Peter Lowy runs his global real estate empire from Aus-tralia.

Reading this book will not suddenly transform a Clark Kent of real estate investing into a land-owning superhero, but it will help you lessen the risks involved in buying and selling property. After all, real estate is—and always has been—a gamble. Every new development is a roll of the dice. Those who have mastered the game understand that it is not Lady Luck who makes the gamble succeed. Rather, it is the ability of the investor to reduce the risk of the game. The goal of this book is to give you the knowledge you need to reduce your risk and stack the odds in your favor. I can think of no better way to get this knowledge than by learning from some of the world's most successful real estate Mavericks—namely, those you are about to meet.

—Steve Bergsman

CHAPTER 1

Make a Good Deal

Finding the right location and lining up
good lenders are some of the easier
aspects to buying real estate. What's tricky
is negotiating a good deal. Patience is a
virtue in the pursuit of getting what you
want. But research, due diligence, planning,
and flexibility are just as important.

When it comes right down to it, the best advice for real estate investors is to practice *patience*. Though there are many instances when it is necessary to act quickly, patience is a virtue even in situations where time is of the essence.

As one case in point, right after the dust cleared from Equity Office Properties' initial public offering in 1997, the real estate investment trust's chairman, Sam Zell, began planning a major expansion. Caught in his crosshairs was another real estate investment trust (REIT), Cornerstone Properties, which he wanted to own.

Zell knew that although Cornerstone had managed to quickly grow its portfolio of properties, the New York–based REIT was smaller and would have trouble gaining access to the capital markets. It took three years, but Zell finally snared his prey, buying the company for $4.6 billion.

The key to this deal was persuading a Dutch pension fund, which owned about 30 percent of Cornerstone, to sell. Although Zell clearly coveted the company's 15 million square feet of office space, much of which was located in the same cities where Equity Office Properties already had a presence, he took his time with the pension fund. "After three years, the timing was right," Zell said.[1]

Convincing the fund to sell was only the first part of the deal. The bigger challenges were ahead. Zell wanted the transaction to take place on his terms, plus he had to convince a group of banks to do the funding. A notoriously tough bargainer, Zell eventually agreed to pay $18 per share in stock and cash in what amounted to adding a 20 percent premium to the stock price at that time.

Equity Office Properties assumed $1.83 billion in Cornerstone debt, but the total price tag amounted to the equivalent of Cornerstone's net asset value—no more, no less.

Since the investment banks were happy to finance the deal, Zell wrangled additional financing, including a $1 billion bridge loan, a $1 billion revolving credit facility, and a $500 million bond offering.

Patience and slow, deliberate negotiations produced for Equity Office Properties a huge addition to its portfolio, along with plenty of capital leeway for anything else Zell might stumble across.

If three years seems like a long time, in the real estate business, it's really not. Hamid Moghadam, president and chief executive officer of San Francisco–based AMB Property Corporation, tells of pursuing a deal for two Kennedy International Airport cargo facilities for two and a half years before nailing down the properties. For Moghadam, it was also a matter of slowly and deliberately convincing the seller to come to the table.

TAKE IT SLOW

There are generally three parts to a real estate deal of any magnitude: coming to a conclusion with the seller, arranging capital from lenders, and—if there are partners—making sure everyone is headed in the same direction. There is no trick to successful negotiating. What works best is knowledge, persistence, and a clear understanding of what everyone wants to accomplish before signing on the dotted line.

Where novices often trip up, even if they find the right real estate in the right location, is falling in love with the property. Pursuit becomes too ardent and clearheadedness disappears. As noted in the Sam Zell and Hamid Moghadam transactions, both were intent on getting their acquisition targets, but neither was compelled to rush into a transaction that was not in his favor.

Most real estate deals eventually collapse when investors spot a potential target—perhaps in a very good location—and feel the need to jump into negotiations under the assumption that someone else might come in to compete in the bidding.

"The worst thing you can possibly do in a deal is seem desperate to make it," says Donald Trump, one of the most celebrated and successful real estate deal makers of them all. "That makes the other guy smell blood, and then you're dead."[2]

This kind of situation puts the buyer entirely at the mercy of the seller, who has his or her own goals and price points in mind. Generally, the seller's goals will infringe on you attaining your goals. And if you don't have strategic goals other than ownership in mind, sometimes it is best to stay out of the market in the first place.

What's also interesting to note about the Zell and Moghadam examples is that the target portfolio and properties weren't for sale until the potential acquirers made inquiries. That is, there was no for-sale sign hung on the front window. In all likelihood, the sellers were not initially happy to see they were the targets of such aggressive buyers. But once they both agreed, everyone got what they wanted.

KNOWLEDGE IS POWER

The discovery of potential targets usually comes about through a combination of industry knowledge and careful due diligence on prospective properties. That is the first step in deal making—either you know the market, you have researched the market, you have performed due diligence on the individual property, or you have done all three.

Angling for the upper hand in any deal requires knowledge,

because in real estate looks can be deceiving. Let's say a three-year-old office building that is 95 percent occupied comes on the market. The handsome property is located in a very hot, suburban real estate market. While it certainly fits a strategic goal, is it really as good as it looks? Suppose three new office buildings are scheduled to come on-line in the next year, or that one of the lead tenants is teetering on the edge of bankruptcy, or that the existing tenants have relatively low leases and, with higher vacancies in surrounding buildings, the likelihood of substantially raising rents remains low. Once you dig deeper and discover these factors, you might conclude that what seems like a good deal is really no bargain at all.

CAREFULLY CRUNCH THE NUMBERS

There is an old negotiating axiom that in a buy-and-sell situation, you shouldn't be the first to state a price. In reality, a workable price will be decided no matter who opens negotiations. The more important point is to decide what form the payment will take and over what period of time before entering into discussions about what you will pay for a property. In addition, if the price being offered is a number that is considerably lower than the seller expects, be able to back up your reasoning for the low bid (the property has serious maintenance issues, competition is rushing to build, etc.).

Donald Trump twists this important point to form a crucial corollary: "Protect the downside and the upside will take care of itself." As Trump notes, he always goes into a deal anticipating the worst. Then, if he can live with the worst-case scenario, the upside should become apparent.[3] That is especially true when calculating financial risk. You have to know whether you will be able to remain standing if the unexpected happens.

It is also important to have a good handle on your financing options before negotiations conclude. Once the seller accepts your bid, you don't want to be scrambling to find capital, which is time-consuming and could endanger the transaction. Although a deal might take weeks or even months to arrange, once everyone is in agreement, it needs to be concluded quickly.

Major deal makers in real estate are generally of like mind when it comes to "squeezing the deal," that is, getting as much as possible from either the seller or lenders. Their collective advice: Don't do it. If your general financial requirements are being met, there is no point in creating hard feelings by trying to get more, because at some point in the future, you could be working with the same folks again on another transaction. This is particularly true if you plan to invest in a number of properties, and especially applies to your dealings with banks (which have very good memories).

"You need to approach every deal as if it is your last," adds Douglas Shorenstein of the Shorenstein Company. "You shouldn't be looking to squeeze the lender, squeeze the broker, squeeze the seller. You may be dealing with most of those people again on another property. You must have a reputation for knowing what you are doing."

John Kukral, president and chief executive officer of Blackstone Real Estate Advisors, a New York–based real estate opportunity fund, claims he spends a lot of time keeping a very good relationship with lenders, trying to understand their business, and learning how he can make their business better for them.

"If I have a transaction that is going to be a clear moneymaker, I don't need to get the last 50 basis points [0.5 percent] out of a loan," he says. "I'm not going to beat up the lender. If this is a great deal, let's get it done quickly. I don't want to spend months negotiating with the lender."

ASK THE RIGHT QUESTIONS

What is interesting about the Zell and Moghadam deals we examined earlier in this chapter is that the sellers did not originally intend to unload their properties. But in most transactions, the seller is motivated, though the motivations are not always clear. Therefore, you should ask the following question: Why does the seller want to unload this particular property or portfolio? Generally, it's not anything sinister. It may be nothing more than the seller needing money to buy another property. Even in situations of desperation, properties for sale are rarely relinquished at highly discounted prices. That is why it's helpful to know the circumstances behind a willing sale. Often a little homework will reveal a bargaining chip that you can use to your advantage.

"What I try to do is work more than anybody so I can understand the asset better," says Blackstone's Kukral. "You have to dig deeper to find something that other people do not know about the asset."

Trump also espouses the concept of "knowing your market," but he claims he doesn't rely on number-crunching researchers. Instead he does his own research on the street because, as he likes to boast, he has the instinct and prefers to draw his own conclusions.[4]

PLAN AHEAD, YET REMAIN FLEXIBLE

After patience and research, the third important part of successful deal making is planning. Deals can be simple or very complicated with a lot of moving parts. The deal should be sketched out from start to finish, including what will happen to the property if your bid is accepted.

Obviously, there are many twists, turns, and bargaining ploys involved in a deal that cannot be planned in advance. Nevertheless, it is important to stay focused on the process and the outcome. There are some intuitive deal makers who can sense the next turn before it happens. The rest of us have to compensate for our lack of intuition by being organized, well planned, anticipatory, and focused.

One of Trump's axioms is to "think big" when approaching a deal. One of the keys to thinking big is "total focus."

By being focused and organized, it is more difficult to fall prey to that must-win-at-all-costs emotion, which generally leads to bad deals. One has to know going in that there are limits to any bid, mostly based on one's liquidity and—for income properties—the ability to recoup the cost through the asset's cash flow. No deal is worth taking on more risk than whatever limits you have initially established—either on paper or through your own intuitiveness.

It is also important to ready a flexible response to the odd twists that sometimes spring up unexpectedly. When Trump was shopping around for property to build his first casino in Atlantic City, he suddenly discovered that Holiday Inn was knocking at his door, wanting to be a partner. Trump didn't feel he needed the big hotel company, nor did he want a partner, but Holiday Inn offered him a deal that was too good to pass up. They would reimburse Trump for the money he had in the transaction, finance all construction, and guarantee him against loss for five years. Instead of owning 100 percent of the project and accepting all the risk, he opted to take 50 percent of the deal without any cost at all. As for the partnership, a few years later Trump bought out Holiday Inn's shares.

Trump, a serial deal maker, says he protects himself by being flexible. "I never get attached to one deal or one approach. I keep a lot of balls in the air because most deals fall out no matter how promising they seem at first."[5]

Trump is also not afraid to drop a deal that is not unfolding to his expectations.

One of his best transactions ever was one in which he seemingly ended up on the losing side. In 1987, Trump set his sights on acquiring Resorts International, an Atlantic City, New Jersey–based hotel and casino owner. His initial move was to acquire $96 million worth of Resorts International Class B stock for $80 million. While this netted him just 12 percent of the company's equity, it gave him 90 percent of the shareholder votes. His intention was to eventually buy the rest of shares and take the company private.[6]

Merv Griffin, the former singer and talk-show host, started playing entrepreneur after his fledging entertainment career cooled down. Seeing a chance to outtrump the Donald, Griffin bid $35 a share for Resorts International, a 60 percent premium over the $22 a share Trump was willing to spend.

Trump knew he couldn't outbid the interloper and negotiated the best bargain he could, selling his shares to Griffin. That netted Trump $12 million. He also got the then-unfinished Taj Mahal casino in Atlantic City as part of the deal.

As for Griffin, he overspent by a wide margin for Resorts International. By 1989, Resorts International's debt service was cruising along at $133 million, but the company's estimated cash flow was under $30 million. Resorts International quickly fell into Chapter 11.[7]

Even Trump knows his financial limitations. He initially let Griffin get the best of him on the Resorts International acquisition. But he was flexible enough to negotiate something out of the transaction, which turned out to be the winning hand in an eventually messy outcome.

It is also important to remember that sometimes you get a second chance. Many deals fall apart for one reason or another. When that happens, sellers and their brokers turn to the next buyer in line. Even deals that come to fruition sometimes go awry for the buyer, meaning the property could turn up on the market again at a better price point down the line.

TAKE CHARGE

While it is important to get good advice—financial, legal, and otherwise—if you really want a deal, you must take the lead in making it happen. As Trump notes, "I do my own negotiating. Generally speaking, it works out much better that way."

Budding real estate entrepreneurs get held back in early deals for a number of psychological reasons: fear of failure, fear of not bidding the appropriate price and terms (the other side of this psychosis is fear of insulting the seller with an inappropriate bid), inability to get the deal in motion, and self-doubt. With so much capital at stake, sudden weakness prevails, and the potential entrepreneur starts soliciting support from family and friends, who know very little about the details of the deal and offer the most conservative advice—often and inadvertently negative.

Again, the only solution is to take charge, stay focused on the deal, and avoid unnecessary distractions.

Failure to complete a deal might not make you rich, but it won't bankrupt you, either, if your only other choice is to conclude a completely unfavorable transaction.

Richard LeFrak is president and chief executive of the Lefrak Organization, one of the largest private real estate companies in New York and the biggest owner of multifamily units in the Big Apple's metro area. He modestly notes that deal making is not his forte. What he and his company do best, he often stresses, is development. Nevertheless, LeFrak has cut some amazing deals over the years.

Twenty years ago, the company made a huge bet on Jersey City, right across the Hudson River from Manhattan. At the time, the area was derelict and home mostly to railroad tracks and old industrial structures. LeFrak sensed that affordable housing and offices would attract residents and customers who were priced out of Manhattan's expensive real estate. LeFrak won't say how much it cost for the 600 acres of Jersey City property he acquired, but admits that with only half of the land developed, he has already recaptured the dollars he spent on land acquisition and construction.

BE TOUGH AND NEGOTIATE HARD

While LeFrak is demure about his deal-making skills, Trump revels in his, which is why he called his first autobiographical tome *The Art of the Deal.* He explains in the opening paragraph of his book, "I don't do it [real estate deals] for the money. I've got enough, much more than I'll ever need. I do it to do it. Deals are my art form."

Years later, as he spoke to me sitting in his opulent New York office, Trump gave new meaning to his term *art of the deal.* "It's having the vision to see where the world is going to be, so when the building is completed they are standing in line to get in."

While Trump emphasizes that he uses different tactics for every deal, the ambiance of his approach is always the same. He is patient, is extremely knowledgeable about the target property and immediate market conditions, can raise capital quickly if needed, and is not shy about ruffling feathers. His style combines equal measures of friendly determination and hovering threats. It is about as edgy as one can get.

"You've got to be tough. You've got to negotiate tough, and you cannot, at any time, let anyone take advantage of you," he says. "As bad as things got for me—and they got pretty bad—I never let anyone push me around. This saved my ass. I always sent out the message: 'Don't lie to me. Don't cheat me. Because I'll find out and I'll find you and it won't be pretty.' "[8]

Not every deal Trump completes works out in the end, but the ride is always thrilling. When he does score, it's generally a grand slam.

When the 72-story number 40 Wall Street was constructed in 1929, it was the tallest building in the world until the Chrysler

Building was erected in 1930. Still an architectural gem, the office tower suffered through decades of mismanagement and ownership uncertainty, all of which Trump observed with an uncanny eye for detail.

In the 1980s, Ferdinand Marcos acquired 40 Wall Street. At the time, Marcos was the Philippine dictator. His chaotic ownership ended when the leasehold interest was acquired by a private investor for a cost north of $100 million. At that point Trump became interested in the property, only to watch a Hong Kong firm, the Kinson Company, buy the building. Kinson poured money into renovating the property, but could not make it profitable. Plus, Kinson was having troubles with its contractors and an avalanche of liens were placed against the building.

In 1995, Kinson hoped to bail out and turned to Trump, asking only $5 million, or $4 a square foot, for a key Wall Street building.[9] Granted, the office market in New York had not fully recovered from the real estate recession of the early 1990s, but it was still an absurdly cheap price for the tower.

Trump determined there were at least $4.5 million in liens and trade payables against the building. If he paid Kinson $5 million, most of that would be used to pay off the problems. Trump figured he could do a better job himself of dealing with the problems, so he offered Kinson $1 million and agreed to assume and negotiate the liens—which he did at a fraction of the outstanding value.

After the ink was dry on the contract, Trump says he was "surprised" to learn that Kinson failed to disclose other claims against the building, which Trump satisfied by deleting those amounts from the postclosing price.

The final purchase price, as Trump loves to boast, was less than $1 million for 1.3 million square feet of Wall Street space. Even with an additional $35 million in renovation costs, 40 Wall Street was one of the best real estate deals in Manhattan since the Dutch bought the island for $25 worth of beads.

MEET THE MAVERICKS

Donald Trump

Birth Date: 1946

Occupation: Chairman and President, The Trump Organization, New York, NY

Education: BS, Wharton School of Finance, University of Pennsylvania

Career Highlights:

- Develops glamorous Trump Tower in New York, which becomes a tourist attraction
- Builds Trump World Tower in New York, the tallest residential building in the world
- Creates Trump Hotels & Casino Resorts
- Buys General Motors Building and 40 Wall Street in New York
- Publishes two best sellers, *The Art of the Deal* and *The Art of the Comeback*

BREAK THE RULES

Trump remains the most unusual of all real estate investors, a true Maverick even as his real estate empire—won then lost then won again—spirals into the billions. At last count, revenues for The Trump Organization jumped past the $10 billion mark.[10] Trump probably has used and abused each rule about real estate investing mentioned in this book more than once. While most other developers specialize in one asset class, Trump seemingly invests in everything, often on a whim. Gathered through storms, his port-folio is stuffed with casinos, apartment buildings, huge mixed-use developments, hotels, golf courses, and country clubs.

A peek into Trump's holdings (including his publicly traded Trump Hotels & Casino Resorts) reveals a hodgepodge of amazing properties and businesses. In New York alone, there are 11 different buildings and projects: Trump Tower (residential and retail), General Motors Building (offices), Trump Place (residential and commercial), Trump International Hotel & Tower (hotel and residential), Trump Parc (residential), Trump Park Avenue (residential), Trump Plaza (residential), Trump Place (residential), 610 Park Avenue (residential), Trump World Tower (residential), and 40 Wall Street (offices). Then there are five casinos, six golf clubs, six resorts and country clubs, and odd items like the Trump Grande Ocean Resort and Residences in Miami, Trump Pageants, and management of the Wollman Skating Rink in New York.

If other wheeler-dealers forge close ties with partners and banks, Trump will do the same. But he is also known to force out partners who disappoint him and squeeze financial sources at crunch time.

Where others play it safe, he prefers to be out on the edge. He's a tough negotiator, who drafts smart, tight contracts and wields attorneys about like army divisions. All the while, he portrays innocence. "My deals are not contentious," he pleads. But somehow they often end up with lawsuits and threats.

Trump lines up partners and frequently finds they do not meet his expectations. After realizing Holiday Inn was not a very good casino manager, he forced a showdown until the company sold out. He then began buying Holiday Inn shares, sending a message that he was flirting with the idea of taking over the entire company.

In 2002, he fought with Conseco, his partner on the 50-story GM building in New York.[11] While Trump got the management contract and his name on the building, Conseco put up all but

$11 million of the $222 million equity in the deal. The squabble became so intense, Trump filed a $1 billion lawsuit against his partner, allegedly for blocking an attempt to buy it out.

A year later, he and American International Group, the huge New York–based insurance company, went at it, with Trump telling the press he was shopping around for a new insurer for his portfolio because AIG's prices were too high. AIG returned the fire, claiming Trump was just acting out because AIG did not buy into a junk-bond deal Trump issued. Eventually, AIG decided it wouldn't offer to renew property coverage on the portfolio anyway.

PLAY THE PRESS

Trump probably was using the press to beat down AIG on pricing, a technique no one does better. Many real estate investors hide from the media, feeling the less the public knows about their deals, the better. Trump, as is his manner, takes the opposite approach. He is always willing to talk. Sure, he loves the limelight, but there is usually a method to his madness. No one plays the press better to make a deal. Getting the word out is one of his key rules in the art of the deal.

In 1974, when Trump was trying to get the city of New York to approve his acquisition of the Commodore Hotel on East 42nd Street, he persuaded the hotel's owners to say they were planning to close the property. Trump then hit the airwaves, arguing that a boarded-up hotel would be a disaster for the Grand Central area of the city.[12]

While Trump can be difficult and contentious, even his adversaries say he is a genius when it comes to making a real estate deal happen. Although it can be a rough ride to be on Trump's team, his banks have been unexpectedly loyal.

Trump's most unique accomplishment is not the glitz, the glamour, and the fact that his name is in the media somewhere in the world almost every day. It is that he is one of the few—if not the only—real estate Mavericks to create a brand name. The fact that the word *Trump* appears on almost all of his properties is not just an ego statement. A Trump building is a product representing a very high-end piece of real estate. The name, he says, means considerable price points above a similar product—and that is especially true for his residential buildings.

"I just try to stay ahead of the curve," he says with uncharacteristic modesty.

Then he adds, "I have the best locations. I have the best buildings, I get great zoning. I get really good financing. I build, sell, and rent. And I get more per square foot than other people."

The Trump Tower has become a tourist attraction in and of itself, with 2.5 million visitors annually, according to Trump's people. How does the company describe the property? As a "Mecca of style and high fashion and an elite sanctuary to some of society's most famous and influential people."

With his comb-over hair, critics often lament Trump's lack of personal style. The same cannot be said for his buildings, which are well designed, handsomely appointed, and carry a host of luxury amenities. His 90-story Trump World Tower across from the United Nations, designed by Costas Kondylis & Associates, received a glowing review from Herbert Mushcamp of the *New York Times,* who proclaimed "it punches through the morbid notion that the Midtown skyline should be forever dominated by two Art Deco skyscrapers."[13]

Like many of today's major real estate mavens, Trump experienced the industry firsthand through his father. Fred Trump built middle-class residential buildings in the New York boroughs of Queens and Brooklyn.

Donald Trump was born in Queens in 1946. After graduating from the New York Military Academy, he attended Fordham University, located in another borough—the Bronx. He then transferred to the Wharton School of Finance at the University of Pennsylvania.

Many get-rich-quick real estate schemes are built around the difficult-to-execute concept of buying foreclosed homes. That is not the way most successful real estate investors operate. But Trump usually goes against the tide. His very first deal involved an FHA-foreclosed property in Cincinnati. Called Swifton Village, the 1,200-unit apartment project originally cost about $12 million to build. Trump and his father placed a minimal bid of $6 million. There wasn't much competition because the project looked like a disaster, with almost 40 percent vacancy, bad tenants, and a scarred appearance.

After winning the bid for the property, the Trumps secured a mortgage for their entire purchase price plus another $100,000 for renovations—meaning they got the property without putting up any of their own money. Fixing the place up ultimately cost $800,000, but it was a great investment. The Trumps were able to make the property attractive, bring in better tenants, and take occupancy to 100 percent.[14] And, oh yes, a few years later they unloaded it for $12 million.

LOOK FOR UNUSUAL OPPORTUNITIES

Trump's name is often linked to Manhattan, and for good reason, given all of his high-profile projects there. But he really didn't arrive in the Big Apple until 1971, after graduating from college. His first significant opportunity came two years later when he noticed that Penn Central Railroad, then in the middle of bankruptcy, wanted to sell its two rail yards on West 30th and West 60th Streets in Manhattan.

The latter was especially attractive because Trump thought he could build middle-income housing on the site, yet it was the former property that turned out to be the gem. The city of New York was looking to build a convention center and Trump was convinced the West 30th yard was a perfect location.

By 1974, Trump says he secured an option to purchase the sites for $62 million with no money down.[15] Four years later, the city decided Trump was right and bought the site from Penn Central, with Trump's compensation being based on his original option to purchase.

It was a mixed triumph, though. Instead of choosing Trump to develop the site, the city and state decided to oversee the work itself. Trump pocketed less than $1 million from the deal. Not a lot, he laments, given all the time and work he put in, but the deal did put his name on the map of Manhattan.

Without question, 1974 was a busy year for young Donald. While he was doing the deal for the Penn Central rail yards, he noticed the company also owned several old hotels in the city that it wanted to unload. The one in the worst condition was the Commodore Hotel, adjacent to Grand Central Station.

While the hotel and the neighboring area were in decline, Trump guessed that its proximity to one of Manhattan's two great rail stations made it a perfect location for a convention hotel. But there were a lot of moving parts to this deal, including financing, arranging tax abatements from the city, and finding a prestigious hotel chain to attach its name to the property.

Trump learned an interesting lesson in deal making during this early transaction. He had his mind set on making the Commodore into a Hyatt, since he knew the hotel chain was interested in establishing a presence in the city. Yet he had a hard time getting the company to come on board. Finally, someone told Trump that if you want to get something done, you have to call the top person in the organization. At Hyatt, that was Jay Pritzger. Trump phoned Pritzger, they met, and Hyatt signed on. As Trump notes, "If you are going to make a deal of any significance, you have to go to the top."[16]

There were two very important features about this deal. First, the location was right. Although it seemed at the time the neighborhood was going downhill, Trump correctly figured that with so much foot traffic emptying out from Grand Central and walking past the site, if he could erect something brilliant, the hotel would sell itself. The second attractive feature was the numbers. In 1974, the hotel's room rate was $20.80 a night. Even at a 40 percent occupancy rate, Trump knew he could break even. Trump figured that after renovations, nightly rates would rise to $48 and he could push occupancy up to the 60 percent range. In reality, when the hotel reopened in 1980, room rates were pegged at $115 a night—and the hotel was quickly able to gain occupancy of 80 percent.[17]

Throughout the 1970s and 1980s, Trump continued to erect great buildings in New York and casinos in Atlantic City while throwing money at odd ventures such as the Trump Shuttle Airline and the New Jersey Generals football team. He was at the top of his game when the real estate recession of the late 1980s hit and took down his empire. By 1990, Trump was facing bankruptcy. He couldn't meet payments on more than $2 billion in loans. In fact, he was $975 million in debt, which he personally had to guarantee.

Trump was able to extricate himself from the financial apocalypse through timely negotiations with his banks to secure emergency financing. Eventually, however, he had to give up much of his empire to get more favorable terms. According to *Forbes,* he lost more than two-thirds of his net worth.

With another boom in real estate in the 1990s, Trump returned to triumph, although his company is still plagued with high debt loads, especially his Trump Hotels & Casino Resorts division. In early 2003, the *Wall Street Journal* reported that Trump's auditors had substantial doubt about the ability of Trump Castle Associates LP, a unit of Trump Hotels & Casino Resorts, to continue as an ongoing concern.

Is Trump concerned about losing his empire for a second time? When I asked him that question, he responded, "Heck no. I'm having a lot of fun."

First-rate real estate Mavericks like Trump truly know how to make great deals. Once they have learned from their mistakes and have nailed down the formula for success, they use it over and over again to keep adding to their holdings.

THE MAVERICK APPROACH TO MAKING A GOOD DEAL

1. Take your time negotiating.
2. Don't fall in love with the property.
3. Never appear to be desperate.
4. Realize that knowledge will give you the upper hand in deal making.
5. Work out the numbers before beginning negotiations.
6. Have your financing all lined up in advance.
7. Don't try to squeeze every last penny out of the deal. It could come back to haunt you later, especially if you deal with the same people in your next transaction.
8. Determine the seller's motivations and use that to your advantage.
9. Sketch out your deal from start to finish.
10. Plan for all eventualities.
11. Stay focused on your goals.
12. Remain flexible and open to unexpected opportunities.
13. Accept responsibility for making deals happen.
14. Be willing to take chances.
15. Have a thick skin.
16. Don't take it personally.

CHAPTER 2

Understand Cycles

Real estate has always been a cyclical investment. There is little anyone can do to change that. As a result, because you cannot accurately predict when the market is about to ebb or flow, it is essential to recognize the signs of change and be ready to act at all times.

When business is stable and expanding, the theorists—like their brethren in the corporate world—are blithely optimistic. During the late 1990s, when the economy was still in bloom and construction companies were busy meeting the demands of expansion, a theory began to percolate through the property markets that while real estate cycles might not end in the United States, they would begin to moderate.

After a brutal downturn in real estate at the end of the 1980s and early 1990s that resulted in a financial crisis serious enough to collapse the savings and loan industry, developers in the 1990s tried to build only enough inventory to meet demand. At the same time, lenders stayed cautious. In addition, with the advent of the Internet, property and market information was more readily available than ever before.

Another popular theory at the time held that the easy availability of information made the real estate markets more efficient, thus allowing developers and lenders to quickly ascertain the status of any particular market and the trendline of any real estate asset class. With all of this information, they maintained, it would be difficult to overbuild or underbuild—in essence the two primary causes of real estate cycles. In reality, it didn't quite work this way.

While residential properties held up pretty well in most parts of the country, the commercial real estate markets fell dramatically into another recessionary period a decade after the last downturn. As Hamid Moghadam, chairman and chief executive of San Francisco–based AMB Property Corporation, observes, "The speed with which this industrial cycle turned down was remarkable. It was much faster than any other cycle in my experience."

In explaining why things changed so quickly, Moghadam turns the information-efficient theory on its head. "There is so much information around and markets have become so much more efficient that the speed at which cycles turn has accelerated."

This century's first real estate downturn—especially in the commercial and high-end residential markets—began in 2001. After scrutinizing office market data, Torto Wheaton Research reported that the real estate sector experienced three separate demand falloffs over the course of the year: the emergence of sublet space as a result of companies pulling back on growth plans; a chain reaction to the pullback that developed into a full-blown recession; and the after-effects of the September 11, 2001, terrorist attacks that weighed heavily on the markets.[1]

One more theory common in real estate circles is that cycles turn every 10 years. There is some basis to this thread of thinking, although the timeline is not perfect. There has been at least one real estate downturn during each of the past four decades—a mild one at the beginning of the 1970s (with a little bump in the mid-1970s), again in the early 1980s, followed by the severe real estate recession at the end of the 1980s and early 1990s, and once again at the turn of this century.

No matter what the theory or the hypotheses about timing the market, the point is that real estate is a cyclical business. No one has yet been able to change that.

The odd thing about real estate cycles is that everyone understands they exist. In fact, there have been reams of academic studies defining the beasts, breaking them down into mathematical equations, charting movements, describing cause and effect, and even predicting how and when they will appear at points in the future. Still, to this day, even the best real estate developers and their lenders often get caught when they least expect it.

There are four phases to a real estate cycle, espouses Glenn Mueller, Ph.D., managing director of real estate research at Legg

Mason Wood Walker and director of capital markets research at Johns Hopkins University: recovery, expansion, hypersupply (more product than currently needed), and recession.[2]

Unfortunately, the expansion phase almost always leads to hypersupply. There are numerous theories about the reasons for this: demand predictions; the need by developers to roll profits into the next investment; liquidity; and, most obviously, exuberance. During the expansion phase, demand appears endless, opportunities abound, indicators turn positive, lenders are funding, and economic factors such as occupancy and rental rates are all heading in the same direction—up.

The truth is, no one wants to be the first to say the game is over, so all participants play the expansion phase to the final knockdown. This precipitates a recession slide, which drags down all the other industrial sectors. Developers are generally leveraged, so risk actually rises during an upturn. That becomes a snowball running downhill as the real estate cycle turns. Property owners suddenly do not have cash and can no longer find financing for new developments or existing troubled properties. All the while, the capital needed to cover the difference between one's loan balance and the value of the properties during a downturn erodes.[3]

When real estate investments fail, they often impact the financial markets. In the worst-case scenario—the recession of the late 1980s and early 1990s—the downturn in real estate led to the near demise of the thrift industry and necessitated intervention by the federal government to bail out the troubled financial markets.

Even the most savvy real estate investors, such as Paul Reichmann and Donald Trump, have been caught by sudden shifts in real estate cycles. Reichmann's Olympia & York Company, valued at $10 billion, collapsed under a mountain of debt in 1992. Donald Trump, too, almost made a visit to bankruptcy court.

UNDERSTAND WHERE YOU ARE IN THE CYCLE

"You have to know where the cycle is going because sometimes between zoning, demolition, and all the different things you need to get a building started, it can takes years to complete a project," says Trump. "You don't want to start a project and then by the time you are really into the market have the market disappear."

To some extent, this is exactly what happened to Trump. By 1990, he was facing the untenable situation of being unable to meet payments to his bank on more than $2 billion of loans. Spiraling toward bankruptcy and close to losing his empire, Trump was able to secure emergency financing, though he had to cede control over most of his real estate empire to the creditor banks.

Both Reichmann and Trump survived in the end. Reichmann was later able to take back a key development in London, which has formed the basis of the Canary Wharf Group, a $317 million real estate company. Trump's holdings are even grander today than a decade ago. According to *Crain's New York,* The Trump Organization, with revenues of more than $10 billion, is the largest private company in the New York metro area.[4]

Trump knew he got caught badly in a down cycle. Although it is not his favorite subject of conversation, he likes to tell the story of the time in 1980 when he was standing proudly in front of Trump Tower—then under construction—and ran into Jerry Speyer, who was head of Tishman Realty. After boasting about how successful preleasing on the building was going, Trump concluded by saying, in his own less-than-self-contained way, it was "a spectacular success." Speyer listened politely, congratulated Trump, and then responded before departing, "Be careful of the markets because when the markets change you could take the best apartment in any building in New York and it's got virtually no sale."[5]

Years later, after some very difficult times, Trump realized Speyer was right.

Even the best and brightest in real estate cannot avoid the sudden shock experienced when real estate markets turn sour, but it is possible to avoid cyclical calamities, though it's admittedly difficult. There are a couple of things to keep in mind when it comes to real estate, especially for those on the development side. First, there is the momentum problem that Trump alluded to. Developments, especially if they are large, generally take years from beginning to end. High-rise office buildings, resorts, malls, and mixed-use developments begin with land purchases, zoning commission visits, and occasional state or local government agency perusal or incentivization. Then, after dancing with lenders and waiting one or two years to get everything in order, it's possible to break ground.

IN DOWN CYCLES, STRING OUT DEVELOPMENT

Building into the throes of a recession is sometimes unavoidable. However, for those who recognize that change is a-coming, it is possible to string out development so it will come on-line when the market is perceived to have changed again. Developer-owners can also use this opportunity to refinance existing loans (a popular move in the recession at the beginning of this century, which occurred in the midst of an extremely low interest rate environment) and line up, as much as possible, new tenants.

Despite tough times, there are always some tenants willing to take advantage of a buyer's market to move into a brand-new structure at low rental rates. Obviously, developers will find it necessary to make concessions as a trade-off to filling new buildings.

ACT QUICKLY WHEN CYCLES BEGIN TO CHANGE

Aggregators of property, such as real estate investment trusts, have numerous options. How successful these moves are depends on how rapid the companies recognize change.

"We identified the cycle very early on," recalls Moghadam. "We called the new downturn in industrial demand in January 2001 after coming off a booming fourth quarter in 2000. A lot of people thought we were alarmists."

CLEAN UP YOUR BALANCE SHEET

Recognizing a coming shift in the tide of real estate investment, Moghadam's AMB refined its strategy. It decided to keep its balance sheet "pristine" and line up a significant amount of capital "capacity." The company also disposed of real estate, taking advantage of a property cycle that favored industrial properties.

During the middle of this latest recession, Moghadam was able to report, "People are paying us a lot of money for industrial property even in this market. We have been net sellers of properties in the United States in the last two years [2001 and 2002] to take advantage of that."

One important move was to quickly address rental rates, which typically take a beating in down cycles. "We led the market in terms of rental rates, getting realistic about the direction, and leasing up space ahead of competitors," Moghadam says. "It was such an efficient adjustment to the coming hard times that, at the beginning of 2003, even as the cycle bounced along the bottom, AMB reported a portfolio occupancy rate in the mid-90 percent range, while the overall United States industrial market lagged by 300 to 500 basis points [3 to 5 percent]."

INVEST AGAINST THE CYCLE

For those with guts and capital, the best way to deal with cycles is to be contracyclical.

In the aftermath of the September 11 terrorist attacks, during a slumping economy and a weakening stock market, Shorenstein Company, an owner and operator of Class A (high-rise) office buildings, made two surprising moves. The company and one of the investment funds it managed acquired the million-square-foot 500 West Monroe office tower on Chicago's West Loop for $250 million. It also paid $154 million for Washington Harbour, a five-acre mixed-use development in the Georgetown section of Washington, D.C. The purchases were made when investment capital for real estate was quiescent because everybody else was sitting on the sidelines.

In the mid-1980s, when U.S. real estate markets drifted into classic hypersupply, Shorenstein pulled back on its investment and development activities. It was a time when the value of Class A office buildings was driven to unrealistic highs. Moving against the prevailing spirit of wild development deals, Shorenstein Company eschewed new construction when the market was at the top of its cycle and instead focused on leasing and managing its existing properties.[6]

Walter Shorenstein, founder of Shorenstein Company, came from the old build-and-hold school of real estate. By the early 1990s, he had built and still owned the highest concentration of office buildings in San Francisco's financial district. "The theory was," he explains, "acquire assets and manage them right. We never sold anything."

Then came the severe downturn of the late 1980s. For the first time, Walter Shorenstein experienced a situation where his holdings actually declined in value. "We decided that the next go-around, if

MEET THE MAVERICKS

Walter Shorenstein

Birth Date: 1915

Occupation: Founder, Shorenstein Company, San Francisco, CA

Education: Pennsylvania State University and University of Pennsylvania, no degree

Career Highlights:

- Buys Milton Meyer & Co. in San Francisco
- Forms The Shorenstein Company from old Milton Meyer firm
- Acquires Bank of America Building in San Francisco
- Forges ties with four institutional partners: IBM, Bechtel, MetLife, and Bank of America
- Becomes largest owner and operator of Class A office buildings in San Francisco

things got better, we would sell. If the cycle indicated it would be better to buy, we would buy."

BUY WHEN CAPITAL IS OUT OF THE MARKET

In the early 1990s, after real estate fell off the face of a cliff, Shorenstein moved to take advantage of what he deemed to be an undervalued market. "In the early 1990s, we were very active buyers," says Douglas Shorenstein. "There was very little capital in the market at the time."[7]

Douglas Shorenstein, who joined his father's company as president in 1983, notes, "We buy at points in time when the capital is out of the market, and we sell when the capital overvalues the real estate fundamentals."[8]

When the markets turned in the mid-1990s and aggregators—particularly the REITs—scrambled to fill portfolios, Shorenstein became an active seller. "From 1996 to mid-1998, the REITs were buying like crazy. Analysts wanted to see the REITs become big. We became active sellers to the REITs," says Douglas Shorenstein.

In 1998, a couple of calamities—a Russian debt default and the Long-Term Capital Management debacle—conspired to smack down the REIT buying spree by closing up the capital markets. Once again, Shorenstein Company began to buy.

That previous September, Walter Shorenstein was inducted into the University of Southern California's Real Estate Hall of Fame. In his brief opening comments, Walter Shorenstein noted, "Having been in the industry for over 50 years, it is my opinion that there is nothing more important in an organization than an understanding of the cycles that affect our industry and the flexibility to respond to them."

After recounting some of the cyclical disasters that impacted investors, REITs, syndicators, and banks, Shorenstein observed: "The common denominator behind all these missteps is the fact that operators with too much access to capital and not enough understanding of market cycles were able to thrive in good times, but they didn't have the structure or stability to last when things turned against them. Caught up in a strong market, they never prepared themselves for downtimes that are the avoidable part of our business."

THINK BIG

Walter Shorenstein built his eponymous company into the largest holder of Class A office space in San Francisco. With the help of son

Douglas, he expanded the company beyond the Bay Area into other large cities across the United States. Today, the privately held Shorenstein Company owns and manages about 25 million square feet of office property. A large portion—8 million square feet—is still located in the San Francisco and Oakland area. The rest can be found in places like New York, Chicago, Miami, Charlotte, Sacramento, Phoenix, Philadelphia, and suburban Boston.[9]

Among its trophy holdings are the Bank of America building in San Francisco, the John Hancock Center and Prudential Plaza in Chicago, 450 Lexington Avenue in New York, and First Union Financial Center in Miami.

There are two histories to the Shorenstein Company. The first round of its entrepreneurial leadership began with Walter Shorenstein, who put the company in its development mode. However, unlike other fast-track developers who built and sold, Walter held on for the long term.

"At one time," Walter Shorenstein muses, "we had 70 to 80 percent of the new buildings in San Francisco."

The second history of the company begins with Douglas Shorenstein's surprise (to him) elevation to the top of his father's company. In 1983, Douglas came home to San Francisco after working as a real estate lawyer in New York. "Just before I came out, my father said, 'I'm going to make you president of the company.' I said, 'We have a president, so that just doesn't make sense,' " Douglas recalls. "I went out of the country, came home, and returned to my office. The telephone rings. It was a reporter saying, 'Gee, I see in a press release you are president of the Shorenstein Group.' I didn't know there was such a thing as the Shorenstein Group." As it turns out, there wasn't!

Two important alterations to the company's way of doing business happened under the stewardship of Douglas Shorenstein. First, it became an acquirer instead of a developer, operating in the manner of private REIT. Second, it made many of its subsequent acquisitions through Shorenstein Company sponsored and managed investment funds—of which the firm was a major investor.

Still, it all began with Walter Shorenstein. Now in his late 80s, the elder Shorenstein continues to report to his office on the 49th floor of the Bank of America building in San Francisco most days. The views of San Francisco Bay from his high perch are so inspirational, they have probably added years to his already long and full life.

The spacious office—about the size of three New York studio apartments—is needed. The walls are covered with awards and photos reflecting a lifetime of hard work. Although he confesses it is better to let son Douglas run the company, he remains busy and has a full-time secretary awaiting his instructions, as always.

His speech patterns, while sure, are less flowing now. He stops, sometimes in midsentence, to get a fix on his thoughts before continuing. Douglas allows his father to ramble on, knowing that a point will be made. It's not that Walter Shorenstein's memory is failing, but after so many years in the business, there are a lot of reminiscences to sort through.

Born in 1915, Shorenstein grew up on Long Island, New York, eventually making his way to Penn State and the University of Pennsylvania, but dropping out before gaining his degree. After serving in the armed services during World War II, he was furloughed in San Francisco around Thanksgiving 1945.

At the time, recently married and with a baby on the way, Walter Shorenstein guessed he could make a fairly good living working in real estate on a commission basis. In 1946, Shorenstein secured a position with a local brokerage firm called Milton Meyer & Company, which mostly dealt in residential properties but had been dabbling in commercial ones as well. Shorenstein did not want to sell homes, so he opted to focus on commercial property, becoming a one-person commercial brokerage department. Five years later, he became a partner in the company. In 1960, he bought the company, keeping the name Milton Meyer into the 1980s when Douglas Shorenstein came on board. That is when the firm's name finally and proudly became Shorenstein Company.

The first building that Milton Meyer acquired after Walter Shorenstein became president was the Merchant Exchange building in San Francisco. It's a good example of how quickly the elder Shorenstein does business.

After talking to friend Ben Swig, a well-known real estate investor, about the difference between being in the brokerage business and owning real estate, Swig suggested that Shorenstein move into ownership, a direction in which Shorenstein was leaning anyway. Swig told Shorenstein the next time he found a good property, he would let him know, and they could become joint owners.

In 1965, the Merchants Exchange building came on the market for $1 million. He and Swig were to commit $500,000 each. But Shorenstein knew that even if they were co-investors, Swig would end up being the dominant partner. So Shorenstein went to a local bank and told the lender, "This would be a good loan for you because Ben Swig is willing to put his real estate brand on it. Could I borrow money from you instead of being in debt to Ben?" The bank's limit was $250,000, which it would lend to Shorenstein if he could come up with the other $250,000. He told an associate at another bank about the deal and how he had already secured the first $250,000. Then he said, "It would be a cinch for you to put up the remaining $250,000." The banker agreed.

"I went to the banks because I didn't want to be beholden to Ben," says Walter Shorenstein. "I had other ideas."

Douglas, born in 1955, was raised in San Francisco. He eventually traveled across the Bay to go to college at the University of California at Berkeley. After getting a law degree from the University of

California Hastings College of the Law, Douglas Shorenstein went to work at a Wall Street law firm, Shearman & Sterling, in its real estate group.

"I pretty much knew I would come into the family business, but the question was how," Douglas Shorenstein says. "After college, I thought it was a good idea to go to another part of the country and get experience. I went for one year and stayed for four. Then my dad put his arm around me, told me I was in danger of becoming a lawyer, and that it was time to come home. This was at the end of 1983."

Two years later, Douglas Shorenstein found himself in the middle of one of the landmark deals of the mid-1980s.

Bank of America was suffering serious financial problems, taking huge loan losses. Its stock tanked and it needed to sell assets to save the company. As a result, its home office, the 1.8-million-square-foot Bank of America building in San Francisco, was put on the block.

"I would never have done this deal," Douglas Shorenstein confesses, "but my father had his eye on the biggest building in the city." Nevertheless, it was up to the younger Shorenstein to run the acquisition process.

HAVE CAPITAL READY TO BUY

Goldman Sachs represented the bank on the deal. For some odd reason, every time it looked like a transaction was cinched, it broke up before completion. On September 13, 1985, Goldman Sachs came to Douglas Shorenstein and said if he could close by the end of September (the bank needed to close a deal by the end of the quarter), the deal was his.

MEET THE MAVERICKS

Douglas Shorenstein

Birth Date: 1955

Occupation: Chairman and Chief Executive Officer, Shorenstein Company, San Francisco, CA

Education: BA, economics, University of California at Berkeley; JD, University of California Hastings College of the Law

Career Highlights:

- Moves Shorenstein Company into financing through closed-end investment funds
- Acquires and develops Oakland City Center
- Acquires John Hancock Center and Prudential Plaza in Chicago
- Portfolio expands to 20 million square feet of U.S. office space
- Makes first investment in loans, buying $20 million junior mezzanine loan from CDC Mortgage Capital Inc.

Using no partners, Shorenstein paid $660 million for the structure, which was the largest single office deal in the country at the time.

"Everybody was perplexed at how we wound up with the building, but it was simply that Bank of America needed to book this deal and they knew we could move quickly," Douglas Shorenstein admits.

"This building gave us a new dimension," adds Walter. "The fact of the matter is we wound up with 25 percent of the multitenant, Class A office buildings in the financial district, about 7 million square feet."

The deal indirectly pointed the Shorenstein Company in a new direction. Douglas Shorenstein realized that for the firm to expand, it would eventually have to look elsewhere in the country. He also knew that new deals would have to be capitalized differently than they were in the past.

Walter Shorenstein was essentially a developer. To finance new projects, he worked with a set group of investors. The idea was, if something came up, he could turn to the investors, get all the financing together quickly, and respond to opportunity. Over the years, Shorenstein developed close ties with four major capital sources: Mutual Benefit Life Insurance, MetLife, International Business Machines, and Bechtel Group, all of which were partners in most of the Milton Meyer developments under Walter Shorenstein.

While that worked through the 1980s, the real estate recession that began later in the decade changed real estate's financial markets for good. A better structure for acquisition needed to be developed.

Douglas Shorenstein is fond of saying that what Shorenstein Company does today is not much different from the way his father operated. It has strong investor relationships to partner in deals, although the deal making is a lot more formalized these days.

In the early 1990s, when Shorenstein Company began to look for new financial partners, all of the life insurance companies had withdrawn from the field. Douglas Shorenstein turned to a new source of potential funds—university endowments, foundations, and high-net-worth individuals—which were generally smart, long-term, and, important for the time, contracyclical investors, not unlike Shorenstein.

In 1992, the company organized and sponsored the first of what would be a series of closed-end investment funds. The initial one raised $150 million, with the Yale Endowment, Shorenstein Company, and four other investors each putting up $25 million.

How were the numbers decided? Partly by happenstance. "Yale asked me how much we were going to invest," Douglas Shorenstein says. "I responded, 'How much are you going to invest?' Yale said it would put up $25 million. I said we would put up $25 million, too. One of my associates was kicking me under the table because, in the fund business, the general partner sponsor historically makes money mainly on fees. But the fees weren't large enough; I wanted to make our money on the equity."

When Shorenstein Company was doing development with its regular set of financial partners, it would always put up the same amount of equity as the partners—placing its dollars in alignment with the investors. "What I was trying to do was mimic the capital relationships my father had in the past," Douglas says. "We put in the same amount of equity as all the other investors. It was the kind of relationship that could be brought into the future."

Shorenstein creates a new fund when the one before it is about 65 percent invested. The amount of capital it raises is targeted to the amount it can invest over a three-year period. In addition, the capital gets leveraged by about 60 percent. The funds are set up for 15 years, though assets may be sold when opportunities arise.[10]

STOCKPILE CAPITAL

By stockpiling capital in funds, Shorenstein Company can, as it has in the past, move quickly when opportunities arise. This allows the firm to invest contracyclically when necessary.

When the real estate recession of the late 1980s drifted into the next decade, the price of commercial real estate began trending downward. By this time Shorenstein Company was about to make an important momentum shift. After finally digesting the Bank of America building, stabilizing the property, and sitting out the real estate bubble of the mid-1980s, the company acquired a 2-million-square-foot portfolio from Beta West (a subsidiary of U.S. West) that included properties not only in San Francisco, but in Denver, Phoenix, and Omaha as well.[11] It used capital from its first investment fund to make this purchase.

Shorenstein Company was able to buy when sellers needed to unload the properties due to lower performance expectations. At the same time, it began its strategic goal of reducing the risk of being in one market by investing across the country. (In the mid-1990s, Shorenstein expanded further by purchasing properties in Charlotte, Nashville, Miami, and the Boston and New York suburbs.)

A decade later, the power of these funds worked its magic once again.

In the wake of the terrorist attacks on September 11, 2001, the investment market for office buildings dwindled. With concerns that downtown office buildings were more prone to terrorist attacks and in sudden need of terrorist insurance coverage, the transactional market—already slowed by a flailing economy—came to a bumpy halt.

Shorenstein Company closed its sixth fund with $609 million in equity in the spring of 2001. When bargains appeared, it was ready to strike. In late 2001 and early 2002, when no one else was buying Class A office buildings, the firm acquired 500 West Monroe in Chicago and Washington Harbour in Washington, D.C. In the summer of 2002, it acquired Two Liberty in Philadelphia and 450 Lexington in New York, totaling about 2 million square feet.

Although the general holding period for a fund's investments is 10 years, sales can occur anytime opportunity strikes. After just a year and a half of holding Washington Harbor, Shorenstein sold the building to investors for $185 million.

WHEN FIRST BIDS FAIL, OPPORTUNITIES ARISE

An interesting note about this deal is that Shorenstein Company was not the intended original buyer of Washington Harbor. Another party bid higher. But after a few months of keeping the transaction tied up, the bidder could not close.

"We were there to do a fast close," says Douglas Shorenstein. "Brokers want to get the highest price on deals, so often someone is ahead of us on the first round. For one reason or another, these deals don't always close and the seller gets one more shot at getting the deal done. We get recommended on the second go-round because brokers know we are going to close."

Shorenstein Company makes a point of not taking advantage of the seller's weakened position. "From the start, we bid the number we are comfortable with," says Douglas Shorenstein. "We have done the up-front work and that's our bid. If the seller comes to us on the second round, we are not going to tie the bid up by trying to negotiate the price down. We close at that price and we do it quickly."

For Shorenstein Company, the availability of capital through investment funds allows it to move quickly, which is also what opportunity funds do. Nevertheless, Douglas Shorenstein would not want his company confused with an opportunity fund. "We are putting our own capital into deals, so we are voting with our capital. We are not just going the way of the opportunity funds."

Douglas Shorenstein adds, "We have been at this a long time and can show a track record, not just as a family business, but as an investment company. We intend on being in this business for the long run."

Shorenstein Company, it should be noted, is the general partner on the funds it promotes. How much it earns as the general partner depends on how the properties perform. Douglas Shorenstein would argue this means his firm is incentivized to generate cash flow, which creates long-term value.

"Our investors, including ourselves, as we are one of the largest investors in the funds, don't want or need short-term liquidity," says Douglas Shorenstein. "Our investors are college endowments, foundations, and high-net-worth individuals [minimum investment $10 million]. They are willing to give up the liquidity aspect of real estate they might get through owning a REIT in exchange for long-term, total return. Also, we can provide larger returns than REITs because we can execute on the residual piece of real estate when we see maximized value."

As one example, when a Canadian bank foreclosed on an Oakland development called City Center in 1996, Shorenstein Company immediately moved in and committed capital on a very fast track. "The bank quickly got comfortable with the fact that we were probably its most real buyer and the deal was done," Douglas Shorenstein says. "We bought a million square feet of office space and empty land for $58.6 million, or $111 per square foot."

The acquisition included six buildings totaling 1.1 million square feet, with options to acquire the City Center Garage and three adjoining parcels from the city of Oakland that could support up to 1.5 million square feet of additional development. In 1999, Shorenstein Company acquired the garage and developed a 487,000-square-foot office building on one of the adjoining parcels, which was completed in April 2002. The entire project acquisition basis as of 2003 was $107,807,000.

This includes seven buildings constructed between 1985 and 2002, containing more than 1.5 million square feet of office space, two garages accommodating a total of 1,800 cars, and options to acquire additional parcels that can support up to 1 million square feet of additional development.

After developing the 487,000-square-foot office building, Shorenstein Company sold 50 percent of that project to a pension system. "This allowed us to pull out all of our invested capital," says Douglas Shorenstein. "Today we own 50 percent of the project with no capital left in the deal."

Shorenstein wryly notes, "We had all of our capital out, so we developed the land for nothing at that point." That is a good thing because, after construction began, the Oakland market started moving in the wrong direction. A big piece of the building was to be leased to Ask Jeeves, an Internet company. But when the building was finished, the Internet company bought out its lease. This had the effect of further reducing Shorenstein Company's construction cost in the building.

Despite a Bay Area market that was weakened severely by the bursting of the Internet and telecom bubbles, the initial 1 million square feet of the City Center was 95 percent leased by early 2003, while the new building was 65 percent full.

BEING PRIVATE HAS ITS ADVANTAGES

Shorenstein Company could have easily gone the way of the REIT, as so many family real estate businesses have before. It has steadfastly resisted this temptation. "In the mid-1980s, everyone was pressuring us to become a REIT, dangling all sorts of goodies," Douglas Shorenstein admits. "And there was some point to it for other companies because the banks couldn't lend enough capital, so the only way to get money was through Wall Street."

For Shorenstein Company the prize of capital wasn't enough. "We took a step back and asked what we were going to gain from becoming a REIT," Walter Shorenstein says. "We are independent operators and like to make our own decisions. We didn't want to make decisions based on Wall Street or what Wall Street thought of us. We didn't need some 28-year-old analyst saying we needed to make 36 cents per share for the quarter when we only made 29 cents."

Still, Douglas Shorenstein admits his company is set up similar to a REIT. "Like REITs, we focus on one asset type [Class A, high-rise office buildings] and we manage and lease all our own properties. We have a large amount of capital that we have discretion over."

The obvious difference between this path and a REIT is that Shorenstein Company is private. "That allows us to move more quickly against capital flow," Douglas Shorenstein adds. "It's very hard for REITs to buy in down markets because the stock market is telling them not to be a buyer."

To which Douglas Shorenstein concludes, "There is no other private real estate investment company in the market that has this platform."

THE MAVERICK APPROACH TO UNDERSTANDING CYCLES

1. Realize that real estate is cyclical.
2. Try to get a reading on where the market cycle is right now.
3. String out the development process in down cycles.
4. Be ready to act quickly when cycles begin to change.
5. When entering a down cycle, clean up your balance sheet.
6. Invest contracyclically (against the cycle).
7. Buy when capital is out of the market.
8. Have financing ready for unexpected buying opportunities.
9. When your first bid fails, and you're not the initial bidder, look for opportunities to step in to take advantage of the situation.

CHAPTER 3

Use Other People's Money

Whether you're buying a home, small
duplex, or large office building, real estate
deals are often highly leveraged. One
reason is that financial institutions are
more than willing to make loans for such
investments. However, loans can be risky,
especially for investment properties. As
a result, one of the best ways to reduce
the risk of carrying debt is to bring on
additional partners.

I previously pointed out that there are three parts to a large real estate transaction: bringing the seller to the table, arranging capital, and getting your partners aligned. This chapter discusses the issue of raising capital and explores some of the techniques the Mavericks use to fund their deals.

There are, of course, many developers and investors who go it alone and have the resources to make investments without needing the financial contribution or expertise of others. There are certainly advantages to this. If the capital goes straight from your pocket to the seller, the deal is completely yours. But the larger the transaction, the more likely you are to need additional investors or loans to get the job done.

Fortunately, despite the cyclical nature of real estate, the lending markets are fairly liquid. There is a bewildering array of products available to someone interested in acquiring property. Somewhere out there is a lender offering permanent and semipermanent loans, construction loans, bridge loans, mezzanine loans, equity financing, second mortgages, FHA and VA loans, jumbo loans, or even reverse mortgages. The trouble is, not all financing is created equal in terms of risk. You could inadvertently end up with the lender as your partner—and that is never a healthy investment situation.

Real estate traditionally is a highly leveraged form of investment, where the investor uses as little of his or her own reserves as possible and either borrows the rest or finds partners to contribute the remaining amount of money. By using leverage, the investor increases the potential for a larger profit against the personal commitment of capital, while at the same time highly elevating the amount of risk in the deal.

In the past, banks and other capital providers promoted this sort of financing by lending as much as 90 percent loan-to-value on a property. When the cycle turned, lenders became more conservative, and loan-to-values dropped down to the 75 to 60 percent range, meaning the investor had to come up with the remaining 25 to 40 percent of capital.

That's why as the real estate cycle began to go south at the turn of the millennium, lenders were suddenly cranking out mezzanine financing, which bridges the gap between debt and the amount of equity supplied by the borrower. Lenders like this type of financing because it is expensive money that they can charge double-digit rates for in return for providing just a small piece of the financing package.

Since all leverage is expensive (banks have to make a profit, too), Maverick real estate investors have traditionally sought other ways to finance projects. Their dictum has always been to use other people's money rather than their own.

As you know by now, Donald Trump understands this rule well. In 1998, he joined forces with Conseco to acquire the GM Tower in Manhattan for the bargain price of $815 million, or $560 a square foot, making it one of the highest prices ever paid for a Manhattan office building at the time. Trump reportedly put up only $11 million of the $222 million equity in the deal. As sometimes happens in partnerships, this relationship soured and the two wound up suing each other in 2001 after Trump's attempt to buy out Conseco's interest in the property fell apart.[1]

KNOW WHEN AND WHY PARTNERSHIPS WORK

Partnerships in one form or another stay popular because they bring less-expensive capital into a deal and diversify the risk. While the entity that forms the partnership doesn't have to pay for capital that is brought to the table through its partners, it does give up a full ownership position in return for this infusion, which can be expensive. But there are also many advantages.

By splitting the investment among participants in a partnership, the forming entity shares in the risk, and the original investor is no longer on the line for the entire loss if the investment fails.

Sometimes one partner has expertise in an area the other partner does not. In a simple case of two friends getting together to buy a small duplex, a good match might be one investor who understands real estate joining forces with another who prefers managing the books.

Partnerships also work in instances where one partner already has ownership in a property or properties and needs to restructure, wants to pull some equity out of the deal, or seeks new capital to expand. Let's say that all of your spare capital is tied up in three small apartment structures. Suddenly, an opportunity comes to buy three more buildings, yet you have no spare cash. A good solution may be to bring in an investment partner to share ownership of the original apartments. The new partner's investment, which goes into your pocket, can be used to pay for the other three buildings. While your ownership interest in the original apartments is diluted, you own the new buildings outright.

Sumitomo Life Realty of New York put this plan into action in 2003. It owned three office buildings on the East Coast, but was looking for a way to pull some capital out of its investment to help its parent company in Japan restructure its balance sheet. The solution was to form a joint venture with Hines Interests of Houston, led by Maverick Jeffrey Hines, allowing the latter to buy an interest in three of those office properties. In creating the partnership, Sumitomo was able to get cash out of its investments, while Hines Interests not only got an investment in three buildings, but also became the property manager.[2]

The other advantage to such a partnership is that the amount of capital invested by the partners doesn't necessarily have to equate to a division of profits, assuming there is one. Interest positions are always negotiated. By taking on a management and leadership role, the general partner can negotiate a higher percentage of interest than it could for taking an investment position alone.

Sometimes the general partner or managing partner contributes only expertise and no capital at all. For instance, you might have friends or relatives looking for a place to park their savings other than in stocks and bonds. They can buy a property and have you manage it in return for a percentage of equity. This happens all the time on a larger scale. Institutional investors contribute capital to large investment pools, which hire managers to oversee the portfolio of properties in return for a percentage of ownership.

COMMINGLED FUNDS

In the 1980s, investors—especially monied groups—increasingly began to spread their capital into nontraditional (beyond stocks and bonds) asset classes such as real estate. At the time, popular partnerships, called *commingled funds,* were put together by investment managers.

The idea behind the early commingled funds was certainly valid. A group of investors would place their capital in some form of group trust that was run by an investment manager. The big strategic advantage of this approach was that investors could easily acquire a diversified portfolio of real estate assets.

Two problems arose in these early partnerships. First, the investment manager did not have any capital at stake and therefore its interests weren't aligned with investors. Second, the investment manager received fees for its services whether the investments were successful or not.

To make matters worse, the 1980s version of commingled funds had no exit strategy. When the real estate markets fell apart at the end of the decade and investors wanted to take their money and run, there was no organized way for them to do so because real estate is not liquid. Even in the best conditions it can take a long time for a property to sell.

Today's partnerships must address these two key issues: alignment of investment management interests with those of the investor and ensuring there is an adequate methodology to liquidate investments and return profits to the investor as needed.

LIMITED PARTNERSHIPS AND SYNDICATIONS

The limited partnership remains the most popular form of real estate partnership, whether among family members, friends, local investors, or multi-billion-dollar real estate concerns. A simple definition of a *limited partnership* would read like this: a partnership in which a single general partner oversees investments for one or more passive limited partners. This structure limits liability for the limited partners to the amount invested. On the other hand, the general partner's liability extends beyond any monetary investment. Investment groups of various kinds, including real estate syndicates, use this manner of ownership, hiring a general partner to make decisions for the group and to accept liability for losses.

Hines Interests is among the many companies that use limited partnerships. In 1998, in one of many such transactions, it formed National Office Partners Limited Partnership with the California Public Employees Retirement System to invest in core office real estate. An entity called Hines National Office Partners Limited Partnership became the general partner, holding investment and asset management discretion.

In the 1970s and 1980s, the term *real estate syndication* was applied to a variety of investor pools, many of which took the form of limited liability corporations. As with other pools, syndication allowed investors—big and small—to pool money with others in a similar financial situation while forwarding control to professional management. The term *syndication* has no precise legal definition, and the obligation of the syndicator to the investment group and the investors to each other is determined by the form of organization.[3]

There are a number of legal and tax considerations with syndications. Prior to the Tax Reform Act of 1986 it was sometimes difficult to tell if investors in syndications were looking for tax benefits or investment returns.

After the 1986 act, tax-driven syndications were eliminated, but there are still a number of syndications out there. Again, as with limited partnerships, management and passive investors are sometimes on different tracks. If management is getting healthy fees, it really has no incentive to divest properties even if the market to sell is ripe and it would be advantageous to book a capital gain.

OPPORTUNITY FUNDS

Investment pools such as those mentioned earlier eventually metamorphosed. In the late 1980s and early 1990s, value-added funds were formed, which eventually became known as *opportunity funds*.

Basically, opportunity funds are pools of capital that invest in real estate over a relatively short holding period, mostly 7 to 10 years.

They take on additional risk, often in the form of leverage, to achieve superior returns. The general minimum internal rate of return for opportunity funds most often bandied about is 20 percent, although there are never any guarantees.

In order to solve the problem of early syndications and commingled funds, organizers of opportunity funds often invest their own money along with the other capital sources. This makes everyone more comfortable because investment interests are aligned.

It is difficult to say when the first opportunity fund was organized, but certainly a hallmark was the Zell-Merrill I real estate opportunity fund in 1988, which raised $409 million of private equity. Zell-Merrill was the brainchild of Maverick Sam Zell, who sensed a lack of investment capital at a time when the federal government was accumulating vast pools of nonperforming real estate loans and properties that it would eventually have to divest back into the market.[4]

ADD VALUE TO TROUBLED PROPERTIES

Zell-Merrill I was organized to take advantage of opportunities in nonperforming loans and real estate, thus the name *opportunity fund*. Such funds often seek out troubled properties that, through professional oversight, can be righted and put back on the market.

"What we really try to do is buy properties where we can add value through active management," says John Kukral, president and chief operating officer of Blackstone Real Estate Advisors, a New York company that raises capital for its own opportunity funds.

There are various estimates regarding how much opportunity funds have raised through the years. Nori Leitz, a managing director of Pension Consulting Alliance, guesses that just over $72 billion was raised through 2000, and estimates for 2003 push the number up to $100 billion. An opportunity fund can then leverage its existing monies by 50 percent, creating a considerable amount of capital that becomes available to buy real estate.[5]

Anyone can put together an opportunity fund, although this segment of the real estate investment market has been dominated by some very big players. Among the earliest participants were Wall Street investment banks Morgan Stanley, Credit Suisse First Boston, and Goldman Sachs; developers turned investors like Shorenstein Company; and a good number of investment and investment management firms, including Apollo Real Estate Advisors, Colony Capital, the Carlyle Group, and the Blackstone Group.

As the real estate sector worked its way out of a recession in the early 1990s, the first opportunity funds were put together to take advantage of distressed pricing caused by a severe downturn in the sector. "Coming out of that recession, there was a lot of low hanging fruit," notes Bill Walton, managing principal of Westbrook Partners. "Of course, not everyone realized it and those that did put together the first opportunity funds, many of which were wildly successful with extremely high returns."[6]

One of the early pioneers in opportunity funds, Colony Capital, put together its first fund, Colony Investors I, in 1991. It raised $250 million to acquire distressed mortgages from the federal government's Resolution Trust Corporation. As markets change, so do objectives. When Colony Capital got around to organizing a second fund in the mid-1990s, raising $625 million, it acquired hard assets, including resorts.[7]

The big opportunity funds attract millions of dollars from institutional investors such as pension funds, but smaller opportunity funds have also been organized with money from well-heeled individuals with wealth to spare. The objective remains the same: Bring together a group of investors with like investment aspirations, put your money alongside theirs, leverage (add debt to) the monies raised, and try to find properties that are not doing well at the moment but with a little investment and a lot of tender loving care should be worth much more when put on the market again.

USE CREATIVE FINANCING

One of the greatest creators and managers of opportunity funds is John Kukral, president and CEO of Blackstone Real Estate Advisors. He is a master at bringing other people's money into real estate transactions.

Back in 1985, Peter Peterson and Stephen Schwarzman took $400,000 and opened a small investment company in New York called the Blackstone Group. Their tiny firm grew into a highly esteemed private investment bank with offices in New York and London. Through 2003, the company raised $24 billion for the purpose of investing in six core areas: private equity, corporate debt, mergers and acquisitions, restructuring and reorganization, alternative assets, and private real estate.

The last unit, now known as Blackstone Real Estate Advisors, invests in the property markets. It didn't become established until 1994 when Peterson and Schwarzman realized that in the years following the real estate recession of the early 1990s, there was good money to be made from investing in properties. They wanted to create a separate investment fund just for that purpose. Blackstone formed its first real estate fund in September 1994 and needed someone with experience to come in and get it invested. Kukral was their man.

Born in 1960 and raised in Chicago, Kukral is one of those bright young college graduates who wandered into the real estate business by accident and never left.

MEET THE MAVERICKS

John Kukral

Birth Date: 1960

Occupation: President and Chief Executive Officer, Blackstone Real Estate Advisors, New York, NY

Education: BS, mechanical engineering, Northwestern University; MBA, Harvard University

Career Highlights:

- Cofounds Blackstone Real Estate Group
- Raises $485 million in 1994 for Blackstone's first fund, BREP I
- Buys Savoy Group of London, a collection of luxury hotels
- Oversees the completion of more than 100 separate transactions valued at $13 billion

After graduating from Northwestern University, Kukral's intention was first to travel and then to work before heading off to medical school. In 1982, after answering an ad at the university's placement center, Kukral was hired by JMB Realty Company in Chicago. On his second day of work, the company sent him to look at some apartments it wanted to buy in Denver.

"Basically from that first day, I was traveling around, looking at real estate, and making some sort of judgment about what we should buy, invest, or sell," says Kukral. "I was having a great time."

Needless to say, Kukral's plans changed and he never made it to medical school.

In the early 1980s, JMB was a good place to get an education on how to invest with other people's money. It was one of the pioneers in the real estate syndication business, raising considerable amounts of dollars through Wall Street. However, following changes in the tax act, the syndication business—much of which was tax-driven—dried up.

In 1985, Kukral went on to get an MBA from Harvard Business School and continued working at JMB, but not in real estate.

From 1987 to 1992, Kukral invested for JMB's partners in assets outside of property. In hindsight, this turned out very well for JMB, especially when the real estate downturn hit home in the early 1990s. JMB was able to sell the non–real estate investments in cellular telephone and cable TV for considerable profits.

By 1992, real estate was again looking cheap, and Kukral was put in charge of investing for Acquisition Partners, an early opportunity fund started by JMB. Unfortunately, that stint did not last too long. Kukral's idea was to buy distressed real estate loans, but JMB was not sure it could do that with the fund because loans technically weren't considered to be real estate. After a few other differences of opinion, Kukral moved on to Colony Capital, a private, international investment firm focused primarily on real estate–related assets. He did not stay long, and soon migrated to Starwood Capital Corporation.

Two years later, he accepted an offer from the Blackstone Group to help cofound what has become Blackstone Real Estate Advisors, one of the largest and most successful investors in global real estate. The firm has completed more than 100 transactions comprising more than 600 individual real estate assets valued at approximately $13 billion.

"What I have tried to do is build a real estate team of real estate professionals. Most of my people have hard-core real estate backgrounds and have not simply migrated from the investment banking or financial side of the business," says Kukral. "Therefore, our vision of what an opportunity fund does might be a little different from others."

CREATE VALUE FROM NEED

All opportunity funds take on more risk in an attempt to deliver higher returns to investors (many funds do this through financial arbitrage). "We find the best real estate we can that needs a lot of active management," Kukral explains. "We create value through active management."

The company's investment strategy is based on identifying well-located institutional-quality properties that suffer from temporary or correctable flaws in tenancy, physical attributes, capital structure, market position, and/or management. By exploiting the pricing inefficiencies inherent in assets of this nature and by employing intensive asset management to correct the identified problems, the company repositions these buildings for subsequent sale at premium prices.

The first opportunity funds of the early 1990s struck at a good time. They had plenty of capital when the environment for raising money was sour.

Today, huge pension funds and endowments constitute the bulk of the major opportunity fund investors. Back then, however, opportunity funds were largely underwritten by corporations and wealthy individuals. Whereas today's opportunity funds often raise more than $1 billion in capital, early funds were relatively small. Blackstone Real Estate Partners I raised $485 million in 1994.

INVEST ALONGSIDE YOUR PARTNERS

What made those opportunity funds different from earlier commingled pools of capital was that sponsors such as Blackstone put their own cash into the kitty. The simple philosophy was, "We are going to place our own money in there and if you want to put some money in with us, go right ahead."

One of the most interesting and difficult deals the first Blackstone fund pulled off was the acquisition of Worldwide Plaza, a multiuse development anchored by a 1.6-million-square-foot office tower on the west side of New York. Deutsche Bank held a $600 million loan on the property, which, Kukral says, was "upside down."

There were four property owners, including a Japanese company and three prominent New York investors. Due to the structure of the leases, three major tenants were given an investment in the building as well.

"This was at a time when every bank was trying to shed nonperforming loans," Kukral recalls. "The actual transaction was easy; we just bought the loan for about $380 million. The restructuring was the complicated part because you had to get all these people to sign off and every one of them had a different objective. One tenant wanted to be on a certain floor, another wanted to give back its floor, and the third had gone bankrupt and wanted out of the lease. The Japanese wanted to wash their hands of the whole thing. Everybody had something different that needed to be done."

On top of all that there was a tax problem. If Blackstone just foreclosed on the loan and extinguished $600 million in debt, investors would have been left with a big tax burden since the building had already been depreciated below the debt balance.

"A lot of the restructurings in the 1990s were done in a manner that provided favorable tax treatment," Kukral says. "In this instance, we were able to come up with a structure that deferred taxes for the previous investors basically for the rest of their lives."

The owners of Worldwide Plaza knew they owed the lender money. The Blackstone fund could have just taken control of the building, so there was some incentive for them to cooperate. Still,

Kukral felt it was better to restructure the loan to meet everyone's agenda.

"I would go from group to group," Kukral reflects. "We were absolutely committed to buying the loan and we wanted to get everything restructured to reduce our risk. That is part of what we do—'de-risk' the transaction. We ended up spending 18 months on the restructuring." Blackstone also managed to lease two vacant floors, filling 60,000 square feet of space.

Was it worth it? The deal was completed in 1996. Two years later it was sold to an office REIT. "We roughly doubled our money," Kukral reveals.

FIND CREATIVE SOLUTIONS FOR COMPLEX PROBLEMS

Blackstone loves deals like this, which require creative solutions to complex situations. The firm boasts about its ability and willingness to source, evaluate, and execute complex transactions. This skill is generally considered to be one of Blackstone's key competitive advantages. These creative solutions are applied to underperforming or improperly capitalized assets, allowing the firm to make investments at attractive valuations and create incremental value in them.

In the Worldwide Plaza deal, figuring out the tax resolution allowed the rest of the restructuring to happen. The lesson in that transaction, says Kukral, is "if you are going to pay the highest price for an investment, you have to dig deeper to find something that other people don't know or don't know how to do."

There are numerous ways to buy real estate, including direct acquisition of the property, buying existing mortgages, or, in some cases, purchasing the company that owns the real estate.

In the mid-1990s, Cadillac Fairview was one of Canada's largest property companies. It had a huge portfolio of quality real estate assets, including many of Canada's most successful regional malls. It was also in serious trouble. Due to excessive debt taken on to complete a 1987 buyout, and complicated by a weakening Canadian economy, Cadillac Fairview was forced into bankruptcy by its lenders in December 1994.

This looked like a good investment opportunity for Blackstone, but even with leverage, it had limited funds for such a large deal. The company knew it also needed to have a Canadian participant involved in the transaction. This was a clear case where it was better to have a partner than to go it alone. A Canadian partner would bring an expertise of the country's real estate market and make the deal more palatable to Canadians who might object to seeing so many prime assets become American owned.

In January 1995, Blackstone and its partner, Ontario Teachers Pension Fund Board, submitted a proposal to recapitalize Cadillac Fairview. This ultimately formed the basis for the company's plan of reorganization.

The initial investment was $10.4 million to acquire an interest in the company's senior credit facility (approximately 90 percent of face value of the debt). When the company was successfully reorganized in July 1995, Blackstone and the pension fund bought $278.3 million of Cadillac Fairview's equity. Two years later they bought an additional $7 million.

This deal gave Blackstone a piece of one of Canada's largest real estate companies, purchased at a time when properties in that country were in a deep, cyclical low.

When Blackstone looks for investments, it tries to do three things: focus on high-quality, well-located assets that would appeal to a wide group of subsequent buyers; identify, through due diligence, all of the factors that might reduce the value of a property (ground leases, preemptive rights, long-term contracts, etc.); and have multiple exit strategies, including private one-off sales, portfolio sales, or even mergers with existing companies.

INVEST STRATEGICALLY

Whether the deal is large or small, Kukral makes sure every transaction helps to serve a strategic goal, such as providing a foothold into a new market, solidifying a bond with an operating partner, or enhancing an existing portfolio.

One of Blackstone's largest and best-known deals was the acquisition of a block of high-profile hotels in the United Kingdom. These weren't just any motels off the interstate, but four of the toniest names in the hotel business—the Savoy, Claridge's, the Berkeley, and the Connaught. Together they constituted four of London's top seven superluxury hotels.

Hotel investments are a little more complicated than other types of real estate such as office buildings or apartments because they involve an operating company (Marriott, Holiday Inn, Sheraton, etc.) that actually runs the investment. Over the years, Blackstone had bought a number of hotel properties, starting with Days Inns, Howard Johnson, and other limited service brands, and progressed up the lodging industry food chain.

In 1998, when Kukral heard this portfolio of hotels was for sale, he immediately hopped on a plane to London to meet with the management team. "We really didn't know much about the hotels or ownership. We just knew these were some very good assets," he admits.

A lot of people thought Kukral was wasting his time, because others had tried over the years to buy these hotels. They were controlled by a family trust, which had never been inclined to sell before. When Kukral arrived in London and met with management and its advisors, he was convinced that this time there would be a sale.

The proud little hotel company had fallen on hard times. It decided to stop paying dividends and used that money to reinvest in its hotels. This move eventually led to the sale. Although it was a public company, many of its shareholders were old family trusts and foundations that had the bulk of their net worth in the stock.

One key point that Kukral and his team discovered: The chain was being upgraded, and a lot of rooms were out of service. He figured if Blackstone did nothing more than finish the renovation and open up all the rooms, cash flow would dramatically increase.

In England, when one tenders an offer for a company, it has to be a fully financed bid, Kukral says. "That means we must have the money before we bid. This requirement made it difficult for others to put in a competing bid." What makes opportunity funds effective is the fact that the cash is there and readily available to use when a buying opportunity arises.

"That's one of the biggest advantages opportunity funds have," Kukral adds. "You can sit down and write a check for large sums of money to get control of transactions. We were there in London, we were financed, we were able to buy it, and we were able to devise structures to minimize taxes for the company."

Blackstone paid $980 million for the quartet of hotels and another smaller property. Blackstone was so comfortable with its first foray into the hotel business that it subsequently went after another high-end property—the Ritz Carlton in Boston. This turned out to be an incredibly successful investment.

The Ritz was put up for public auction. Although Blackstone did its homework on the property and figured it could solve the hotel's problems (which were physical and tax-related), Kukral didn't want anyone to know he was bidding. "We knew if I or any of my partners showed up at the auction, the competition would know we had done our homework and would bid a dollar more than us every time," Kukral explains.

Blackstone actually used a ruse. It sent a new employee, a junior associate, along with a lawyer to do the bidding. They kept in contact with Kukral by cell phone.

"The very morning of the auction one of our potential competitors called, saying, 'There are only going to be two buyers. Why should we bid against each other? Let's split the transaction,'" Kukral recalls. "But we had done so much work on this hotel, we felt we could easily be the successful bidder."

At $75 million, Blackstone was indeed the winning bidder. "Afterward, when the competitor found out the unidentified guy who won the bid was actually bidding for me, he was very upset, telling the press that Blackstone had done a huge disservice to its investors because it could have gotten the hotel $10 million cheaper if we had worked together."

Two months later the property was sold for $125 million. That was a case where there would have been one partner too many. "We would have had to share half those profits with the competition," Kukral laughs.

Actually, the sale of the Boston Ritz Carlton was part of a much larger deal. Just before the end of 1998, Blackstone completed the sale of its controlling interest in 12 luxury hotels (including the Ritz Carlton Boston) and a mortgage interest in the Four Seasons Beverly Hills to Host Marriott Corporation. The sale price was $1.2 billion, with Blackstone receiving, among other benefits, net proceeds consisting of 40.2 million operating partnership (OP) units (unregistered stock that is not taxable until registered) in the newly formed Host Marriott REIT, equating to approximately a 16 percent equity interest in the company. Almost three years later, Blackstone completed its third and final block trade, with Salomon Smith Barney selling its remaining shares of Host Marriott Corporation.

What's interesting about Blackstone as an entity is that, although it has created four investment funds through 2003—raising about $4 billion in the process and always adding new investors—for the most part, the core investors have not changed since the first fund began back in 1994. Those original investors have stayed with the company and even today form the bulk of any new fund's capital.

PARTNERS SHOULD BE ACTIVE MANAGERS

"We look at ourselves as an operating company, because we manage our properties ourselves," says Kukral. "We have a whole group of asset managers and property managers. Our philosophy is that nobody takes better care of the asset than the owner, so any significant asset we operate ourselves."

Over time, by just growing and acquiring assets, not taking the profits and reinvesting, Blackstone would come to be one of the top four or five office companies in the world and one of the top three hotel companies today.

"We are an $8 billion asset company," says Kukral. "Five years from now we probably will be an $8 billion asset company, but we will have all kinds of different assets. We buy, create value, sell, buy other assets, create value, and sell. Then we do it all over again."

THE MAVERICK APPROACH TO USING OTHER PEOPLE'S MONEY

1. Know that there are a limitless number of fund-raising options available to real estate investors.
2. Reduce leverage and risk by using a partnership structure.
3. Avoid expensive debt.
4. Have multiple exit strategies in place.
5. Align interests by making sure everyone contributes capital.
6. Look for opportunities in troubled properties.
7. Creatively solve complex problems.
8. When necessary, join forces with someone who has expertise in an area that you do not.
9. Seek to get extra equity without putting up additional capital by taking on a role in managing the property.
10. Create value for sellers by addressing their financial needs (e.g., solving a tax problem).
11. Focus on high-quality assets that others will want to be involved with.
12. Identify the factors that might reduce a property's value on the front end.
13. Raise money before you need it so you can act right away on opportunities that others don't have the cash to take advantage of.

CHAPTER 4

Establish Cash Flow Targets

When acquiring existing buildings or rentals, savvy investors look for properties providing solid current cash flows. With new projects, developers plan carefully to make sure they will achieve their cash flow targets as soon as possible.

In 2001, Canada's O&Y Real Estate Investment Trust was capitalized through a $150 million initial public offering, along with an equal amount of financing from O&Y Properties Corporation, a Philip Reichmann company. With secure financial footing, O&Y REIT set out on the acquisition trail. One of the first deals made by the company ended up, purposely, being somewhat complicated. It bought an economic interest in First Canadian Place, a Toronto office complex, by advancing a $55 million participating loan to O&Y Properties.

The loan, in turn, gave O&Y REIT a piece of First Canadian Place. It bore an interest rate of 11 percent. In addition, O&Y REIT was entitled to 25 percent of O&Y Properties' annual cash flow before debt service from First Canadian Place exceeding $40 million.

The term *cash flow* remains a tricky little devil to pin down. Everyone believes in it, and O&Y REIT wanted a piece of it, but cash flow is often defined differently by each company that touts its importance.

Mack-Cali Realty, the big New Jersey–based office REIT, uses a pretty simple definition: the owner's rental revenues from the property less all property operating expenses. In this case, cash flow ignores depreciation and amortization expenses, as well as interest on loans to finance the property.[1]

UNDERSTAND THE CONCEPT OF CASH FLOW

The importance of cash flow is that it is a generally understood data point that can be used to evaluate performance for any type of transaction, acquisition, initial financing, or even refinancing. Cash flow—along with the cost of financing, taxes, and other encumbrances—can have a significant impact on the financial performance of a piece of real estate, which is why everyone follows it so closely.

Donald Trump, in his usual Trumpian manner, declares, "You have to consider cash flow the ultimate. If you don't understand cash flow, you can't count on selling your property at a profit."

New players to real estate investment should not be put off by the complex notion of cash flow. Once you understand the basic concept, all other calculations relating to it are rather easily performed.

Besides, it is no longer difficult to calculate cash flow. Numerous software products on the market, all of which tout similar benefits, calculate rates of return, rent levels, future value, and even the best year to sell the property.

CASH FLOW IS INTEGRAL TO ANY DEAL

Whether buying or selling, cash flow calculations should be a key factor in the reasoning behind any transaction.

Shorenstein Company likes to bring properties to market when they show good cash flow because it adds to the price. "We buy an asset, stabilize it, and create cash flow," says Douglas Shorenstein, chairman and chief executive officer of the San Francisco–based firm.

Cash flow can be a factor on the buy side as well. "We tend to value properties on the cash flow side," Shorenstein explains. "If we can't cover our debt on the cash flow of a property, we won't buy it."[2]

Sometimes, the ability for a property to achieve adequate cash flow can be a deal breaker—or maker.

Soon after September 11, 2001, Blackstone Real Estate Advisors, through one of its funds, acquired a large hotel company for almost $800 million. "If you think about the environment back then, everybody was worried about another [terrorist] event happening," says John Kukral, president and chief executive officer of Blackstone Real Estate. "They said, 'How could you buy hotels in this environment?' "

The answer was in the details. "We got the seller to take back $140 million of zero-coupon financing. So if the cash flow was there, we paid it. If not, we didn't have to pay. It was obvious that we could survive a downturn and still hold onto the asset."

KNOW THE LENDING FACTORS

Generally, mortgage lenders look at three factors when evaluating a loan request:

1. *The most important factor is the loan-to-value ratio.* If all of the lender's criteria are met, the maximum dollar amount of the loan can be ascertained. Low loan-to-value amounts mean the loan or borrower is less than ideal.[3]
2. *A second parameter is the type of property.* Office buildings, apartments, and shopping centers all have different, inherent risk factors that increase or decrease depending on market conditions. One determination of loan eligibility is whether the property could be easily disposed of if there were to be a default.[4]
3. *The third parameter is cash value.* The cash flow or income potential of a property can be used as collateral. If the property is producing cash flow after all expenses and the property income can cover monthly expenses, monthly payments can be made without the borrower having to reach into his or her pocket. This adds a greater degree of safety to the note for the lender.[5]

MAKE CASH FLOW IMPROVEMENT A GOAL

In 2002, Corporate Office Properties Trust, a Columbia, Maryland–based REIT, acquired a two-building, 290,245-square-foot office complex in Chantilly, Virginia (in the Baltimore/Washington, D.C., corridor). The price tag was $48 million.

The transaction included the right to purchase a six-acre, fully entitled development parcel that could support 83,000 square feet of additional office space. As Corporate Office Properties' president and chief operating officer Randall M. Griffin noted at the time of the deal, "Our strategy is to capture this growth over time through capitalizing on our ability to develop another 780,000 square feet of office space on the 56 entitled acres that we now own or control." The strategy easily aligned with the company's stated acquisition goal: Achieve high cash flow yields over the long term without taking undue risk.[6]

Investors who actively acquire real estate are looking for specific things: yield and/or appreciation. Yield investors prefer to own a stable property that continues to throw off a predictable and steady income stream. Capital investors look for the appreciation inherent in the property itself. However, if one can improve the yield, the inherent value of the property appreciates quicker. That is why a lot of opportunistic investors try to find properties that have the potential for upside through an added building, low rental structures that could be improved, stabilization of unstable or weak occupancy situations, and so forth.

In a real sense, the objective is to juice cash flows.

In discussing his company, Great Lakes REIT chairman and chief executive officer Richard May explains the interrelationship of data points such as occupancy with cash flow this way: Every 1 percent increase in occupancy will equate to about $0.05 per share in cash flow growth for us. Today, our occupancy stands at 84 percent, but our normal occupancy rate is 93 percent. As the economy recovers and occupancies return to historical levels, we should add $0.45 cash flow per share. In addition, we have been increasing our cash flow growth internally, through rental increase and improved operations."[7]

There is no one-to-one relationship between increased rent or occupancy and cash flow because formulas or software that figure this equation have to take into account a number of extrinsic factors. This is not to say that increasing rent rolls will not have a dramatic effect on cash flow.

In 2001, Torto Wheaton Research did a study of market fundamentals among REITs. It concluded that a 5.3 percent annual rent growth on average to those REITs represented in the NAREIT Office Index would translate into cash flow growth of 9 percent. For the industrial sector, Torto Wheaton figured a 3 percent rise in rent growth would produce an 8 percent cash flow growth rate.[8]

CASH FLOW IS A MARKET SIGNAL

As noted, opportunistic investors try to create value over a relatively short period of time. In investment terms, that could end up being five to seven years. This, of course, means finding properties with upside potential that can be realized through renovation and better management to help create excellent cash flow. At the point when cash flow is at a peak, opportunistic investors sell, generally to yield investors looking for that steady return.

Changes in cash flow over an entire sector generally indicate the turning of a cycle. More often than not, the leading indicator is the apartment group. The reason is that apartment leases are of a much shorter duration than office, industrial, and retail leases. Therefore, they are much more responsive to a changing economy.

In 2002, during the heart of the U.S. recession, a study by Reis Inc., a New York real estate research firm, reported that cash flows at apartment buildings had begun to decline the year before, while the average cash flows at office buildings remained flat or increased slightly through the same year. Reis said about the offices, "With above-market leases beginning to burn off, cash flow dropped. We've had four consecutive quarters of declining rents and rising vacancies. The weight of those two stones has finally been enough to push down the actual dollars flowing into the buildings."[9]

DON'T PLAY WITH CASH FLOWS

Although cash flow is such a ubiquitous data point, investors often find unique, if not disastrous, ways to use it.

Many have raised capital by borrowing against cash flow. This is a risky play, especially if the real estate cycle begins to turn.

The problem in a downturn is that many investors have leveraged their cash flow. If investors borrow 80 percent against what they perceive to be current cash flow and a failing market unexpectedly takes a bite of it, that debt becomes underwater.

Anthony Deering, chairman, president, and chief executive officer of The Rouse Company, sometimes uses the hot REIT market of the mid-1990s as a treatise on the misuse of cash flow. As Deering notes, in the mid-1990s REITs were an innovative idea that produced a lot of fees and got overly promoted. Because investors wanted high dividend yields and private owners of the companies that were going public wanted maximum proceeds, dividends were pushed to the extreme. "Many IPOs," he says, "promised dividends that not only were substantially more than the required 95 percent of net earnings, but represented 100 percent, even 120 percent of net cash flow. It's one thing to pay out all your earnings, but quite a different matter to pay out more cash than your operations are generating."[10]

It was obvious that this high-payout model was not going to work. As Deering suggested, one way to beat that particular problem was to increase cash flow while holding down dividend growth. The question was, how do you grow if you are paying out all the cash flow? The answer in the mid-1990s was to sell more stock.[11]

PUT CASH FLOW IN PERSPECTIVE

To Stuart Hornery, cash flow dependence smacks of accountant dependence, and he wants none of either—especially when it comes to development.

Hornery knows what he's talking about. In 1978, he became managing director of a well-respected but relatively small Australian property company called Lend Lease Corporation. He built it into a global giant before retiring from the business some 20 years later.

"I keep accountants as far away from development as humanly possible," says the still ornery Hornery. "I have never been a proponent of internal rates of return. This isn't to say that you do not do cash flow targets throughout, but when you talk about development it is much more about making sure your research is right, your intuition is right, your presale is good, and you have execution bottled down 100 percent so you have predictability of outcome."

Companies should do cash flow analysis, he adds, "but it's about doing all those other things in addition to looking at cash flow targets."

Hornery, who uses the terms *cash flow* and *internal rate of return* interchangeably, says even in a nondevelopment context it can be misleading. "I observe these days that if somebody says they have an internal rate of return of 15 percent, people think that is guaranteed."

That is the danger. Quoted cash flow is just a moment-in-time data point. Tomorrow, cash flow (i.e., internal rate of return) could be 25 percent or 5 percent. "You need to look behind the cash flow to see what is going to support it," says Hornery. "These days a lot of attention is given to spread sheets and pro forma at a time when things change quickly."

While it's true investors rely heavily on cash flow, Hornery suggests some investors mistakenly form an opinion based on those numbers when they really should be making a judgment call about the integrity of the trendlines that are producing those numbers. "I'm not saying cash flow numbers are not a useful tool," Hornery notes, "but it is not a panacea. It is just another thing that has to be looked at."

Indeed, investment performance can be measured using a variety of methodologies. The most popular, besides cash flow, include sales comparisons, net present value, and discount and capitalization rate performance.

If cash flow has to be used, Hornery, in another blast at accountants, declares, "I'm much more interested in a property professional doing it than having some outside accounting person do it."

Dick Dusseldorp, the founder of Lend Lease, is considered to be a legendary figure in the world of Australian business. As an immigrant to Australia, he created what has become one of the largest real estate companies in the world. At last count, sales for Sydney-based Lend Lease Corporation Limited tallied more than $8 billion.

That is a legacy from someone who had lived in his new country less than a decade before floating on the Australian stock market one of the country's first post–World War II property development ventures. Dusseldorp died in 2000 at the age of 81.

Less legendary, but no less important to the history of Lend Lease Corporation, is Stuart Hornery. He was elevated to president of the company at the tender age of 38. The year 2000 was important for

Lend Lease in another regard. That is when Hornery retired as chairman of the company after 22 years.

In 1978, when Hornery became the company's managing director and Dusseldorp moved to the chairmanship position (Dusseldorp retired in 1988), Lend Lease earned $15 million after taxes and boasted a market capitalization of $140 million. When Hornery retired, the company was valued at more than $8 billion.

Today, Lend Lease provides a full spectrum of real estate and real estate–related services, ranging from investment management to commercial credit services, development, financing, construction, and project management. The company likes to say it has two core business platforms: real estate investments and real estate solutions. This also describes the firm's two overarching goals.

In real estate investments, Lend Lease is one of the largest real estate investment managers in the world, with $51.8 billion of assets under management. Lend Lease's investment programs cross the risk-return spectrum for both equity and debt capital, in both the public and private markets.

Lend Lease's Real Estate Solutions business offers property-related services to clients involved in the creation, improvement, or management of real estate assets. This consists of development and capital raising, program management, project and construction management, design, engineering, and facilities and asset management across all sectors. The business includes Bovis Lend Lease, a leading worldwide construction and project manager; Actus Lend Lease, a developer and manager of U.S. military housing; and Delfin Lend Lease, one of Australia's largest residential/urban community developers.

In addition, GPT Management Limited, a subsidiary of Lend Lease, manages and is custodian of the assets of General Property Trust, Australia's largest diversified listed property trust (Australia's version of a REIT), with assets of A$6.7 billion.

Lend Lease set up General Property Trust in 1971 to get real estate off its balance sheet. The first property it acquired was a Lend Lease regional shopping center in Penrith, Australia. GPT is a separately listed company, but, as noted, is managed by Lend Lease.

Lend Lease itself is complicated, but as with most global ventures, it started off in a much simpler and local way.

Dick (real name Gerardus Jozef) Dusseldorp was born in the Dutch city of Utrecht in 1918. As a teenager, he enrolled in his home city's Middelbaar Technische School to get a degree in civil engineering. During the occupation of the Netherlands in World War II, Dusseldorp was rounded up and deported to Germany for forced labor. He escaped and made his way back to Utrecht.[12]

After World War II, Dusseldorp joined Bredero's Building Company of Utrecht. By 1947, he was the firm's construction manager. Four years later, as a senior manager with Bredero's United Companies, he was sent to Australia to evaluate the country for business opportunities. He liked what he saw, and Bredero's Australian operation, Civil & Civic Contractors, commenced operations in 1952.

The Dutch were busy in geographically nearby Indonesia (a former colony) but decided to look at Australia, which was in a postwar building boom, Hornery explains. "Civil & Civic won a contract to build several hundred homes, and that is how it started."

Although Civil & Civic were basically builders, Dusseldorp could see that the bigger business was in development. This took capital and the parent company was somewhat reluctant to go that route in Australia. So Dusseldorp devised a solution. He created a new company called Lend Lease, sponsored by Civil & Civic, and took it public. (Ironically, Lend Lease later ended up acquiring Civil & Civic.)

Dusseldorp decided he would create his own finance and investment company that would lend money in order to build and lease property. With Australia's capital markets then relatively undeveloped,

MEET THE MAVERICKS

Dick Dusseldorp

Birth Date: 1918 (died in 2000)

Occupation: Founder, Chief Executive, and Chairman, Lend
Lease Corporation Limited, Sydney, Australia

Education: Civil engineering degree, Middlebaar Technische
School, Utrecht, Netherlands; Advanced
Management Program, Harvard Business School

Career Highlights:

- Head of Civil & Civic Contractors in Sydney, Australia
- Wins contract to help develop Sydney Opera House
- Builds Sydney's first modern office building, Caltex House
- Key contractor in developing Canberra, Australia's capital city
- Creates Lend Lease Corporation and takes it public

there was only one way to get his hands on sufficient funds for the type and scale of the operation he had in mind—go to the public equity markets and sell shares to investors.[13]

Dusseldorp understood that he would still have to raise debt from banks and life insurers for individual development projects, but an injection of funds from the public would supplement the more traditional sources of capital, giving him greater leverage, flexibility, and control.[14]

One of the key financial factors in Lend Lease's early success was a large investment by MLC, an Australian insurance company, which subsequently became a major Lend Lease customer. (In the early 1980s, Lend Lease acquired the parent company of MLC.)

When Lend Lease began listing on the Sydney Stock Exchange, its shares immediately jumped 20 percent.

The main reason Lend Lease launched so enthusiastically was that Dusseldorp was known as a man who accomplished great deeds. In the 1950s, Dusseldorp's Australian accomplishments were huge: He developed the first concrete skyscraper, Caltex House, in Sydney; he built the foundations for the Sydney Opera House; and he played a major role in the development of Canberra, the country's capital city.

In the early 1970s, Dusseldorp decided to take his company out of the Sydney office market (it had been one of the first major office developers, with the Caltex House), sensing that it would be a buyer's market for some time. His comments at the time were prescient for the Australia property market, but in the wider world, usefully epigrammatic for all investors. Noting that some operators in the office market would end up going broke, Dusseldorp concluded, "The art is [knowing] what not to be in."

Unlike Dusseldorp, Hornery is a native Australian. Born in 1939 and raised in a small bush town called Muswellbrook, he eventually made his way to the big city of Sydney to attend the university, attaining a degree in civil engineering. Hornery's first job after college was with Lend Lease. After three years, he went to work in Holland with Bredero in the nascent field of information technologies.

Three years later Hornery returned to Australia; three years after that (are you noticing a trend here?), he found himself managing Civil & Civic, which at the time was the largest subsidiary of Lend Lease.

In 1977, Hornery became general manager of Lend Lease and was really just learning the ropes when the company's chief executive died. Suddenly, at the age of 38, he was the company's chief executive.

MEET THE MAVERICKS

Stuart Hornery

Birth Date: 1939

Occupation: Chief Executive and Chairman, Lend Lease Corporation Limited (retired); Chairman of The Hornery Institute (established by Lend Lease shareholders and employees upon his retirement)

Education: BSc (technology), civil engineering, University of New South Wales

Career Highlights:

- Becomes chief executive of Lend Lease at age 38
- Acquires MLC, which provides the platform for Lend Lease's successful entry into financial services
- Builds Riverside office tower in Brisbane
- Develops Bluewater commercial development in the United Kingdom
- Establishes the ACTU–Lend Lease Foundation, a joint venture between Lend Lease and the Australian unions to encourage young people to acquire skills
- Grows Lend Lease into a multi-billion-dollar global company

"I had not done anything in the way of development or asset management," says Hornery. "What I knew about real estate apart from building was zero."

Fortunately, he had a good teacher. Dusseldorp remained chairman of the company and held that position until he retired in 1988.

"He was a good hand-holder," Hornery says. "I earned my good reputation with a lot of help from him."

Hornery had to cut his teeth on development. He did so beyond Sydney and the usual Lend Lease venues.

"Australia at the time was a very small economy, so the company began by doing only one thing: building. All the activity was really concentrated in just two cities—Melbourne and Sydney," explains Hornery. "The thinking at the time was that we should have a reasonable share of all aspects of property, so we became an integrated company. We became a developer, project manager, property manager, and asset manager."

Hornery had spent some time in Brisbane, which was still considered a bit country—not yet one of Australia's fastest-growing cities—and decided to erect a large office building there. "I have always been one to do good research, and I identified this location along the river," Hornery recalls. "But we had to acquire 35 different properties, which we did." Called Riverside, the 42-story, 550,000-square-foot building "was and is still the best office development in Brisbane," Hornery boasts.

The most important expansion to happen under Hornery's watch was the acquisition of the insurance firm MLC. This provided the platform for Lend Lease's successful entry into financial services, which was a significant contributor to Lend Lease profit in subsequent years. He later turned his mind to the continued internationalization of the company.

Dusseldorp, says Hornery, was always keener on the United States than on Australia. It was a much bigger market. For a while, Lend Lease had a joint venture with a United Kingdom bank that provided financing for residential development in the United States. Starting about the 1960s, Lend Lease was doing residential projects in places like Colorado, Texas, and Florida.

When the Australian building boom started imploding in the late

1970s, Hornery had to pull back and concentrate on Australia. It wasn't until the 1990s that Lend Lease expanded overseas in a big way. By the time Hornery retired as chairman, the company had created a huge real estate investment and funds management division in the United States—mostly built by acquisitions. Companies in the stable include ERE, Yarmouth, AMRESCO, and Boston Financial Group.

"The charter was to replicate what we had in Australia, and it was I who decided at that time we would focus first on the United States," Hornery says.

In 2000, when Hornery retired, the firm's real estate investments and funds under management in the United States totaled just over $40 billion—four times the amount in Australia. That number has remained fairly constant ever since.

In addition, Lend Lease had full real estate operations in Europe and Asia. Geographically, A$58 million of Lend Lease's operating profit came from operations in the Americas, A$50.7 million from Europe, and A$34 million from Asia Pacific during the most recent period. Using another statistic, the internationalization of Lend Lease is even more apparent. In 2002, the company reported that $38.4 billion of its global assets under management were located in North America, A$11.8 billion in Australia, $1 billion in Asia, and £2 billion in Europe. Even in its corporate report, Lend Lease reports in three currencies: U.S. dollars, Australian dollars (A$), and British pounds. Lend Lease now operates in 43 countries on six continents.

Among the developments Hornery is most proud of was one of the last big projects of his career. Not well known in the United States, the 1.6-million-square-foot shopping experience called Bluewater in the United Kingdom is probably the most successful shopping mall in Europe. Lend Lease refers to it as "Europe's largest and most innovative retail and leisure destination." It opened in 1999 and changed the face of retailing in the United Kingdom. The mall averages 80,000 visitors a day, not bad considering the average visitor spends three hours there. "It is the largest shopping center in the world by value, not square footage," says Hornery. He guesses the value of the development today is about $3 billion.

One of the reasons Bluewater stands out as a landmark is because it's fairly unique. There are few such creatures as a regional malls in England. The regional mall development is not well liked because it severely impacts a country's little villages and towns. The concept itself was a no-brainer, Hornery says, because its location has a population of 10 million within an hour's drive.

To get this project done, Hornery commuted every six weeks from Sydney to London. He met with community groups and political parties. Lend Lease ran focus groups. By the time the research was all done, the company had interviewed 35,000 people about what they would like in a shopping center.

The trick was to get the best retailers from the start. The big U.K. department store John Lewis was inked first, followed by House of Fraser and Marks & Spencer.

"It was a process," Hornery explains. "You do a lot research. We ran the usual numerics, we talked with a lot of retailers and people in the community, so we had a pretty good idea of what we had to do. It wasn't that the project carried no risk, but there wasn't anything Lend Lease could not deliver."

However, to trim its financial risk on the front end it sold an interest to Prudential PLC. "They did their own independent review and initial assessment," Hornery says, "which was good because you can always convince yourself to do anything."

Today, Bluewater is jointly owned by Lend Lease Europe Ltd. and the Lend Lease Retail Partnership. The partnership was launched in 1999 and has provided a number of institutional investors the opportunity to invest in Bluewater through the acquisition of shares in the partnership. At the beginning of 2003, Lend Lease held 30 percent of the direct ownership of Bluewater. However, the operator of the Lend Lease Retail Partnership is Lend Lease Real Estate Investments Limited.

"The reputation we established at Bluewater immediately began to pay dividends," Hornery says, because the company picked up contracts to redevelop town centers in the British Midlands and Scotland.

If Bluewater wasn't a big enough assignment in recent years, Lend Lease in Australia also took the contract to develop the Olympic Village for the summer games of 2000. And, in the United States, Bovis Lend Lease completed the cleanup of the World Trade Center after the September 2001 terrorist attacks.

CONCENTRATE ON STRUCTURAL COSTS

When taking on ground-up development, cash flow targets are way down on the list of importance, Hornery maintains. "The things that I looked for, besides location, were related to structure. Was it the best and simplest to execute? Did we have the best design? Did we have the best people on the project? Was line management doing its job? Were we executing? How were we doing in preleasing? There were also targets that needed to be met."

Experience, Hornery adds, should tell you where you stand before you start a project. "If you have a shopping center, you know what the going rate of rents for department stores are going to be, and the difference in rental rates between the big and small shops. And, if you come from a building background, you have a handle on what things will cost and whether the project will be developed in a certain time frame."

CHOOSE PEOPLE OVER NUMBERS

Good companies succeed by having good people, Hornery says. Lend Lease was able to transform itself into a global firm because it attracted bright, hardworking people.

"I was never one for MBAs, at least compared to learning in the school of hard knocks," Hornery says. "We were always a young company. I was chief executive before the age of 40 and we had all sorts of executives of equivalent age, in their 30s and 40s rather than 50s and 60s. There was a lot more energy and a little less wisdom. That was the trade-off. You give them responsibility within the corporate guidelines and make sure they execute."

Hornery handpicked his team for the Bluewater project, which was almost entirely Aussies "because that was what I had," he recalls. "Then I hand-selected a number of Europeans to go sit beside the Aussies. It was all a cultural mismatch for a while, but after several years we now have good European managers with the Lend Lease culture."

The willingness of Lend Lease to elevate people with potential, from the moment when Dick Dusseldorp plucked a young Stuart Hornery to be chief executive, continues today. Until May 2003, the person sitting in the chairperson's office was Jill Ker Conway, a historian, educator, writer, and businesswoman.

Born in Hillston, New South Wales, she resided in the Australian outback until the age of 11. After moving to Sydney, she eventually graduated from the University of Sydney and moved to the United States, where she received her Ph.D. from Harvard University. In 1975, she became the first woman president of Smith College in Massachusetts. In Australia, she is well known as a writer, in particular for the best-selling autobiography of her youth, *The Road from Coorain.*

Along the way, Conway became a trustee of the College Retirement Equity Fund and then a board member of Merrill Lynch, where she chaired the compensation committee. Eventually she joined other boards such as Colgate Palmolive and Nike. While Lend Lease was building up its organization in the United States, Jill Ker Conway served as chairperson of Lend Lease U.S. and its property business board.

In 2000, the multifaceted Jill Ker Conway became chairperson of Lend Lease.

As she noted in her first address to shareholders, "It's a tall order to move from the face-to-face community in which our founder, Dick Dusseldorp, developed his beliefs about the relationship between employees, clients, shareholders, and the communities in which we work—beliefs that have been the key to Lend Lease entrepreneurial spirit, because they have linked the growth of employee knowledge of the business and share ownership to the provision of super service to clients."[15]

Perhaps it was super service that led New York City to appoint Bovis Lend Lease as the lead contractor to oversee the entire recovery, debris removal, demolition, and construction of temporary structures on the 16-acre site where the World Trade Center stood before the terrorist attacks of September 11, 2001.

That was probably the high point of Conway's tenure as chairperson of Lend Lease. After only two years as head of Lend Lease and after being a director for 11 years, Conway stepped down, as Lend Lease, like all real estate firms, suffered in the global recession that arrived with the new millennium.

"Lend Lease has always been a great real estate company, and the difficulties we have experienced in execution of the global real estate investment management strategy over these past years are a great personal disappointment to me," said Conway. And probably to

Hornery as well, since Lend Lease, over the course of 2002 and 2003, opted to reduce its global presence, selling off a large portion of its real estate service companies in the United States. Even its share in the Bluewater mall in England is up for sale.

"We firmly believed in the opportunity to globalize Lend Lease's two businesses—real estate solutions and real estate investment management," said Conway as she left the company. "Whilst the real estate solutions business is in an extremely strong position because of that strategy, we have fallen short of our objectives for real estate investments."

Why the change in Lend Lease's global strategy? Apparently, as Hornery feared, the moguls have given way to the accountants. David Crawford, who spent his whole professional career working in Australia with the accounting firm KPMG and headed Lend Lease's Audit Committee, replaced Jill Ker Conway as chairperson.

The rationale of change was best mouthed by Lend Lease Group CEO Greg Clarke, who explained: "One of the things that I find about running a global business is that global businesses are hard to run because you have different time zones, different tax regimes, you have different languages, you have different business cultures, you have different regulatory regimes."

Crawford and Clark decided it was not worth the effort to be an international company anymore. "We were spending too much money trying to harvest cost synergies—huge IT systems, for example, that weren't yielding, which could measure benefits that didn't exist," Clark opined. "So we've been stripping out complexity, we've been stripping out initiatives, we've been simplifying our business and focusing."

THE MAVERICK APPROACH TO ESTABLISHING CASH FLOW TARGETS

1. Understand the concept of cash flow and how it impacts the bottom line.
2. Cash flow should be a key factor in determining whether you buy or sell a property.
3. Juicy cash flows can help to pump up returns for both yield and appreciation.
4. Industrywide declines in cash flow are usually a signal that more serious market problems are ahead.
5. Don't become overdependent on cash flow. Other factors can be just as important.
6. Concentrate on numbers other than expected cash flow when evaluating a new development.
7. Often, bringing in better management will help to create better numbers.

CHAPTER 5

Be in Alignment

Any decision to buy property must be aligned with your overall intentions and operating strategy. The best and easiest way to stay in alignment is to specialize in one specific asset class.

"In the end you have to know your product better than anyone else." Those strong words came from Walter Shorenstein in a speech he gave while being inducted into the University of Southern California Real Estate Hall of Fame.

"In addition, you must have partners that recognize your expertise and are willing to rely on your recommendations," he said. "They may bring other kinds of business skills to the table, but you must bring a knowledge of your product and market that they will respect."

A decision to invest in real estate, whether it is to buy and hold or to develop literally from the ground up, should be based on something more than the expectation that the property will produce profits. Successful real estate investors and developers understand there are no sure property investments. Therefore, the way to reduce risk is to thoroughly understand your markets and your product.

ALIGN INVESTMENTS WITH YOUR OPERATING STRATEGY

To begin with, in any type of real estate investment transaction, you must align your overall intentions with your general operating strategy. In other words, there has to be operational justification for the purchase, beyond profit. Sure, you should approach any investment with dollar signs dancing in your head. But to make money, you must stay focused on the business, on the strategy, and on the operational plans.

Along these lines, don't get caught in a personal war with the seller. The objective is not to beat the person on the other side of the table. Rather, it is to make sure that what he or she has to offer fits your investment or corporate needs.

"There is no secret to good real estate investment other than to stay focused," says Doug Shorenstein, president of San Francisco–based Shorenstein Company and Walter Shorenstein's son.

STAY FOCUSED AND INVOLVED

Real estate investors who get singed by their investments often allow others to handle the nitty-gritty of the deal or management of the property. They want to buy a piece of land or a building, step back, and let the wealth accumulate like cherries growing on a cherry tree. That might work if you are in a partnership with others experienced in these matters—or if you are getting paid to manage the property—but it is not likely. In fact, property managers have an enviable position, since they are paid whether the investments succeed or not.

Individuals who build strong, ongoing real estate concerns always remain part of the process. The late Sam LeFrak, whose Lefrak Organization pioneered massive middle-class housing developments in New York City, used to say, "We have a hands-on policy. I can tell you what's going on with every fragment of this company."[1]

HAVE A STRATEGIC GOAL

Part of being in alignment is simply having an eventual goal and knowing what it will take to achieve that goal. Even in a basic, speculative purchase, you want to acquire land with the eventual goal of selling it at a significantly higher price. To evaluate your chances of reaching this goal, you must ask several key questions. If you are borrowing the money, what is the cost of capital? Can you maintain the loan payments, even if you must hold on to the land for years? Can taxes on the land be reduced by using the land for agriculture? Is the land protected from outsiders? What are the market conditions that should lead developers to want this piece of land? If the market turns, will your land still be worth as much as you paid for it?

Individual investors who move into development fall into the category of single-market, entrepreneurial developers. They build projects, borrow the construction capital, and strive to create significant economic value for themselves and their families. Typically, individual investors hold onto their developments for a long time.

At the other end of the investment spectrum—a long way from the land speculator or entrepreneurial developer—are the professional investors who consistently stay in the market and corporations in the business of real estate. The key is to remain focused on one slice of the market. Diversification is good geographically, but not by product type.

The Lefrak Organization, which has been around for almost 100 years as a family real estate company, eventually became known for its development of middle-class housing. It stayed with that asset class even when times changed. James LeFrak, the company's managing director, notes that while the company remained committed to affordable urban housing, "What changed over the years is the scale of the individual projects. Communities used to be six stories with 100 units. Now our bread and butter consists of communities that are 36 stories and 5,000 units."[2]

Times changed but the niche and the expertise in that niche remained the same.

"Our focus has always been to be very focused and to know everything we can know about one narrow niche in real estate market—urban high-rise," says Donald Shorenstein. "You pretty much know what you are going to see, and there is not a lot we see now that we haven't seen at some point in the past."

BE A SPECIALIST

The best and easiest way to achieve alignment of strategy and investment is to create a real estate specialty. While diversification is the proper goal in personal investment, it is not the best methodology in real estate. This is particularly true when approaching lenders.

Lenders trust investors who function in one asset class, because they can easily discern a dedication and knowledge to all of the ramifications involved in that asset class, whether it be residential housing or distribution facilities. Wall Street is almost emphatic about doing business with those who toil in a single asset class. That is why most real estate investment trusts, which have to return to Wall Street to raise capital, focus on single-asset-class structures.

Of the 174 publicly traded REITs, as listed by the National Association of Real Estate Investment Trusts, only 19 are considered diversified. On an equity market capitalization basis, the total value of all REITs is $159 billion, of which just $12.5 billion belongs to the diversified REITs.

If one throws private REITs into the mix, about 300 REITs operate in the United States. Even the private REITs specialize, although there can be diversification within the asset class. Shopping-center REITs may invest in strip centers, power centers, neighborhood shopping centers, or urban mixed-use redevelopment. (However, mall REITs generally do not do shopping centers of any type, and vice versa.) Health care REITs, on the other hand, might be involved exclusively in medical office buildings, nursing homes, assisted living centers, or acute-care facilities.

DIVERSIFY GEOGRAPHICALLY

REITs are rewarded by Wall Street analysts when they are geographically diversified, because to some extent cyclical turns in the market do not happen evenly across the country. The East Coast could drop into a downturn a year or two before the West. Most individual investors and many family-owned companies remain regional in their investment strategies, generally because they do not have the resources, abilities, infrastructure, knowledge, or time to spread investments across cities or states. That is not necessarily a bad thing. It is better for a small investor to concentrate limited resources on a particular geographic area, as it is necessary to gain expertise in one type of asset. But once you build your assets, geographic diversification can get you to the next level.

By knowing your product best—and devising a development formula that can be replicated almost anywhere—capital sources and other development partners will lean on your expertise. It is often harder to get that kind of respect when throwing up an office building one day and a restaurant pad the next. Focus is crucial.

Even some of the smartest real estate investors took a long time to learn this lesson. Such was the case with Hamid Moghadam, founder of AMB Corporation, an industrial REIT.

Before Moghadam and his colleagues created AMB, he ran a real estate advisory firm that worked with institutional clients. In the late 1980s, as the once hot real estate market began to cool, Moghadam made what he likes to say was "a really good macro call." Even though office buildings accounted for over half of his company's portfolio, he felt the product had been overbuilt, and with the market turning, things were only going to get worse.

Moghadam took money out of office buildings and switched his clients into neighborhood shopping centers and industrial facilities. His feeling—especially for neighborhood shopping centers—was

MEET THE MAVERICKS

Hamid Moghadam

Birth Date: 1956

Occupation: Chairman of the Board and Chief Executive, AMB Property Corporation, San Francisco, CA

Education: SB, SM, engineering, Massachusetts Institute of Technology; MBA, Stanford University

Career Highlights:

- Cofounds AMB Property Corporation
- Converts institutional portfolio of properties into REIT
- Redevelops San Francisco pier, which becomes corporate headquarters
- Coins phrase "High Throughput Distribution" for certain kinds of distribution building

that they did not offer as much appreciation, but they sported higher yields and stability and would do well going forward.

"We felt the market was going to go through a shockwave and we wanted to have nonglamorous, nontrophy properties in our portfolio," he shares. "Neighborhood shopping centers and industrial centers were the epitome of that, so we loaded up the portfolio with these two property types. Sure enough, in the late 1980s and early 1990s these were the only property types that really survived."

Moghadam held onto both the combined retail and industrial portfolio throughout the decade until he and his partners took their company public in 1997. Then, in 1999, Moghadam sold retail properties to concentrate on industrial holdings.

"Initially, we were primarily office, with a minority investment in retail and industrial," Moghadam recalls. "Then we got rid of the office and focused on retail and industrial. When we went public we were one-third retail and two-thirds industrial. After we went public, we sold the retail division to Burnham Pacific Properties—a retail REIT—and California Public Employees Retirement System (CALPERS)."

The decision to sell retail was based on operational and long-term growth goals. In regard to the latter, Moghadam assumed that with the Wal-Marts of the world coming into the grocery business, as well as the advent of Internet shopping, retail in the future would be negatively impacted. The Wal-Mart part of the equation has definitely played out. So far, the Internet impact has not been great, but Moghadam predicts that over the next decade it could account for as much as 15 percent of total retail sales.

FOCUS ON ONE PROPERTY TYPE

Operationally, Moghadam says, the initial reasoning "was unstated at the time, but has now become much more apparent to us as we became focused on industrial. That is, being focused on one product type is really the way to go. I didn't used to believe this, but we have really changed our mind. We have become a much better company now that we are focused on one property type."

Moghadam has refined the one-product-type philosophy even further. Industrial properties encompass a wide group of buildings—warehouses, distribution centers, and manufacturing plants, to name a few. Moghadam centered AMB's business around High Throughput Distribution® facilities (a phrase he coined), which are essentially distribution buildings that move goods in and out as quickly as possible. The idea is that these facilities benefit from the growth in global trade and the expedited movement of goods. They are strategically located near airports, seaports, and interstate highways in key distribution markets across the United States, Mexico, Europe, and Asia.

It is an interesting shift, although few companies follow this same line of thinking. Certainly, AMB is the only publicly traded industrial REIT moving in that direction. However, this doesn't mean Moghadam is moving into risky territory. He admits he has made a few wrong bets in his professional life, but those were just bumps in the road. He has built AMB into the second largest public holder of industrial real estate in the United States. As of the end of 2002, AMB owned and operated 94.6 million square feet of space in 992 buildings spread across 30 markets.

BE UNASSUMING

Like many other real estate entrepreneurs, Hamid Moghadam got a taste for the business from his father, a high-rise apartment builder in Iran. "I used to go around with him on the weekends and look at projects, walk the construction sites, and things of that nature," Moghadam says. "In kindergarten and elementary school, when people asked kids what they wanted to be, and others said policeman or fireman, I said I wanted to be a builder."

Moghadam is not tall, but he is stocky. His movements are smooth, and everything about him seems self-contained. Neither his demeanor nor his conversation is as aggressive as that of most developers. In a world where great real estate moguls have been known to be hard-driving, ego-driven, and acerbic, Moghadam is just the opposite— polite, friendly, and analytical. A stranger meeting Moghadam for the first time might guess him to be a college professor.

His cubicle in San Francisco is small and almost unadorned. He shares some of his workspace with his assistant. If he were not so wealthy from his successful real estate endeavors, he could easily slip into the medieval role of a scholarly monk.

Moghadam was born in 1956. He went to school in Iran until he was 13, at which time he was shipped off to boarding school in Switzerland. He eventually came to the United States for college. He earned undergraduate and graduate engineering degrees from the Massachusetts Institute of Technology and an MBA from Stanford University.

"I went to Stanford Business School when the revolution was starting in Iran, and I knew I would not be going back," Moghadam says. "I thought a business-oriented background would be needed in the real estate business."

One of Moghadam's earliest jobs after university life was working for a former Stanford professor who had pioneered the concept of a real estate investment advisory firm. Three years later, in 1983, Moghadam and his associate, Doug Abbey, decided to form their own company. About a year later, when Bob Burke joined the firm, it became known as AMB (the initials of their last names).

From 1983 to 1985, AMB provided a wide range of real estate consulting and advisory services to investors and corporations. One of its first major clients was the Clorox Corporation, which had a headquarters building in Oakland. AMB helped Clorox restructure its lease and ownership structure for its headquarters. The deal was the subject of a Stanford Business School case.

At the beginning of 1985, AMB made its first significant change—transforming into an investment advisory business and securing its first institutional client, the estate of James Campbell, a large private trust based in Hawaii. The estate needed to diversity its property holdings from the islands to the mainland.

With the real estate market sinking fast in the late 1980s, AMB began taking over management of real estate assets from investors who had fallen on hard times. At the same time, institutional investors began hiring the company to turn their investment funds around.

The decision to eschew high-rise office buildings and move into neighborhood shopping centers caught a lot of attention. In the lean real estate years of 1989 through 1991, AMB was able to raise considerable money from such institutional investors as California Public Employees' Retirement System, California State Teachers Retirement System, and Southern Company. By sponsoring commingled funds, AMB quickly moved from raising $20 to $30 million a year in new capital to raising $200 to $300 million.

By the late 1990s, the company had accumulated about $3 billion of assets under management and decided to go public. It was a gutsy call, because this type of offering had not been done before. AMB became the first company to convert an institutional portfolio owned by pension funds into a REIT. It did this by rolling the assets into a private REIT and taking the whole thing public.

The assets combined with the management company became the publicly traded AMB Property Corporation.

"We had to get everyone's okay," Moghadam says. "We got more than 90 percent participation from our private investors." The few investors who either did not like the transaction or could not act quickly enough to include their interests into the deal essentially got cashed out or transferred their assets.

Unlike AMB, most firms that went public as REITs were originally developers with a lot of leverage that survived the downturn of the early 1990s and needed a vehicle for re-equitizing their businesses. In those days, says Moghadam, the joke was they either had to go public or go broke.

AMB continues to operate somewhat uniquely, especially in regard to raising capital. When Wall Street looks kindly upon the publicly traded real estate sector, most REITs turn to their investment bankers to raise capital, which can be done in a number of ways, the most common being to issue more equity.

From Moghadam's point of view, companies that raise money exclusively in the public markets have a major disadvantage: Their equity never becomes scarce. This means investors are less likely to pay a premium for those companies. After all, they know that as soon as the company issues new shares, it will result in a dilution of share value.

One aspect of AMB's business that Moghadam does not mind boasting about is that it "has never raised money on Wall Street beyond our IPO," which is to say, after the company's initial public offering, AMB never indulged any secondary equity offerings, selling additional shares to raise capital.

Since its initial public offering, AMB has gone in the opposite direction of most REITs by retiring more than 6 million shares of stock through buybacks.

PRIVATE CAPITAL IS A GOOD SOURCE OF FUNDING

Instead of issuing stock, AMB turns to private sector capital sources. Since its IPO, the company has raised more than $700 million in private capital from such institutional investors as pension funds, endowments, and foundations.

AMB can't completely turn its back on public capital. It has issued preferred stock and raised public debt from capital markets. But the company's singularity can be attributed to the fact that its franchise remains private capital funding—that is, from third-party, institutional investors. "There are very few REITs that actually do this," Moghadam says.

Since selling its retail portfolio, AMB has remained focused on the industrial side. There is really no high visibility to this asset class, but other features make it interesting—including high cash flows, low capital expenditures, and high predictability. Industrial properties have higher cash flows because items such as capital expenditures, tenant improvements, and leasing commissions that fall to the bottom line are generally lower for these properties compared to other real estate assets. Industrial properties tend not to get overbuilt as quickly as office buildings. Since industrial construction is relatively rapid, when market supply starts to get out of whack with demand, new construction easily can be shut down.

For Moghadam, there is another attraction to this asset class: Tenants use the same industrial developer in different locations. "There is a lot of repeat business with the same customers, particularly when you specialize in one aspect of industrial, which is what we have done," Moghadam says.

A look at AMB's top 25 customers illustrates this trend. The company holds 30 leases with the U.S. government and FedEx Corporation, 12 leases with Los Angeles County, 9 leases with CNF, and 7 leases with International Paper, Ahold NV, Danzas AEI International, and Forward Air.

Not all of Moghadam's ventures have been successful. His belief that the Internet would eventually weigh in more heavily in retail induced him to invest an estimated $5 million in Webvan, an Internet grocery service launched by Borders Books & Music cofounder Louis Borders, in 1999. In addition, Webvan leased more than a million square feet of distribution space from AMB in a number of separate facilities. Like many other Internet experiments, Webvan failed. During the first quarter of 2001, AMB wrote off 93 percent of its investment in Webvan, totaling $4.7 million.

"Markets change, and we are by no means perfect," Moghadam admits. "Our goal is to get 60 to 70 percent of the decisions right. This is a tough business."

To which he adds, "We are really in a business of singles and doubles. In a typical year we invest $500 million to $750 million, and that might be 50 separate transactions or 100 to 200 different buildings. Even if you get some guesses wrong, it is not going to kill you. If you were in the business of buying a $200 million office building and you guessed wrong, that could really hurt."

Obviously, Moghadam does not mind a bit of uncertainty. That willingness led AMB to create one of its most celebrated and unique developments—unusual in the sense that it is more of an office building than an industrial facility. This deviation from the company's stated investment norm is quite forgiving, since the new building was to become AMB's corporate headquarters.

As a shipping gateway to the Far East, San Francisco has historically experienced considerable construction along its extensive waterfront. This dates back to 1932, when Pier 1 was constructed as the 90,000-square-foot warehouse and headquarters for C&H Sugar Refining Corporation. The building was dominated by a massive, sculptured, arched entrance that faced San Francisco's Embarcadero, which is the frontage road linking all waterfront piers.[3]

In the early 1960s, when container shipping replaced loose freight on the world's oceans, C&H closed the facility. It sat vacant until 1965, when it suffered the fate of most unused real estate: It became a parking garage.

More than 30 years later, San Francisco formed a Waterfront Land Use Plan to create a blueprint for future improvements. That is when AMB turned its attention to the area. "We were looking for a home for our company, and we really liked what was happening to the waterfront," Moghadam says.

In a sense, the potential redevelopment of Pier 1 was not so different from what AMB did in the industrial world by redeveloping transportation facilities in major urban markets.

When the building attained a listing on the National Register of

Historic Buildings, redevelopment became feasible because the developer could get a 20 percent restoration tax credit, representing a good chunk of savings on a $42 million renovation.

GOVERNMENT REGULATIONS
ARE MERELY A HINDRANCE

The downside was that any project would need government clearance. In fact, more than 20 separate government agencies had to review the project, enough to dismay any developer.[4] Also, new pilings and infrastructure on the pier were needed and eventually would cost $7 million.

"People saw it and realized they could not go through the legal requirements to convert the property," Moghadam says. "We spent a lot of time on it and did a very sensitive redevelopment plan, making sure to meet all of the historical preservation, coastal commission, and maritime requirements. We had to be very patient, but we thought the prize at the end of the day was worth the effort."

AMB had something else in its favor. The Port of San Francisco had to move out of its headquarters in the city's Ferry Building and needed a new place to settle down. It chose Pier 1.

Pier 1 opened in December 2000 as a two-story office building with 151,000 square feet of space sitting on a 770-foot-long bulkhead.

"There were three or four other companies in the running for the project," says Moghadam, "but what really put us in a good position was the fact that we were committed to moving our own headquarters into the building, and we are a major employer in San Francisco."

Perhaps AMB is best known for advocating a strategy that even more narrowly defines the industrial asset class. Moghadam espouses the theory that the industrial business is going to split into two extremes: storage and High Throughput Distribution. He wants to be in the latter.

It's not that Moghadam doesn't like storage—it is merely a question of long-term value. If goods are going to sit in a warehouse for a long period of time before being shipped, that facility could be built anywhere. If it houses products that are not rapidly distributed, it might as well be built where a customer pays the cheapest rent.

In contrast, High Throughput Distribution is designed for goods that move quickly. Speed is a necessity in today's business world and a crucial driver of competitive advantage. The need for speed creates a demand for properties that can expedite the distribution of goods throughout the supply chain.

"The idea stems from looking at inventories in the economy over a 50-year period," Moghadam explains. "The ratio of inventories to economic output or final sales has declined, which means people are getting better at utilizing inventory that is moving more quickly through the supply chain. If goods are sitting in a warehouse, it is costing you money."

Moghadam stresses that, in today's marketplace, transport companies need facilities designed for speed, not storage.

For a site to be an effective high-throughput facility it should have high door-to-floor ratios, adequate truck courts, good access, and shallow depths. AMB also maintains that the best high-throughput facilities need to be in major metropolitan areas, close to distribution hubs such as airports and seaports.

High-throughput facilities are also tied to the rapid distribution of goods from around the world. So much product is coming into the United States from overseas, it reinforces the concept that good high-throughput facilities should be located near ports or international airports—both of which are AMB's preferred sites.

Today, AMB is the largest nonairline owner of industrial property at the world's busiest cargo airports. Customers here are serviced through AMB's dedicated Airport Facilities Group, a division that focuses on airport and airport-adjacent properties in targeted global hubs and gateway markets.

The company's biggest concentration of on-tarmac facilities can be found in Los Angeles, San Francisco, Seattle, Chicago, New Jersey/New York, Atlanta, and Dallas. AMB has facilities in other cities, but all of its on-tarmac properties make up only 8 percent of the portfolio. A big part of these holdings came in a large acquisition the company made in late 2000 when it bought 95 percent of 20 on-airport cargo facilities located at eight U.S. airports. Aviation Facilities Company sold the portfolio to AMB for $99.5 million.

In many of AMB's desired locations, relatively little land is left for new buildings, creating a barrier to entry. For example, Moghadam likes the area around the port of Los Angeles/Long Beach, which is surrounded by a metro area of almost 15 million people. However, there is almost no developable land left near the ports. "You cannot build another five buildings there unless you knock something down and build in its place," says Moghadam.

HAVE PATIENCE

Moghadam is extremely practiced in the exercise of patience. This has served the company well, not only in the building of his corporate offices in San Francisco, but also in other real estate deals elsewhere around the country.

The Halmar Group, a New York developer of commercial buildings, owned two cargo buildings at Kennedy International Airport in New York. The structures had what Moghadam considered to be a perfect location, and he coveted them.

"They were located inside the fence at JFK, right on the tarmac, so airplanes could actually pull up to these buildings," says Moghadam. "That is the ultimate location, because there is no more of that space available today."

It took two years, but AMB finally convinced Halmar Group to sell. With 31 buildings, AMB now owns one-fourth of the warehouse and distribution space around JFK Airport.[5]

Deals generally come down to pricing and economics. The Kennedy Airport transaction eventually worked for two other reasons. Halmar was concerned about its employees, so AMB ended up retaining some of them. That was a good thing, because they proved to be qualified, competent, and valuable in running this real estate. At the same time, Halmar knew it would be able to sell the property only to someone approved by the airport. AMB certainly fit that bill.

A GOOD REPUTATION GOES A LONG WAY

"Building a reputation and niche in this business is as important as having a competitive advantage," Moghadam says. Reputation is also important with customers, which is why they often ask AMB to expand with them across the country and overseas. To meet this demand, the company created a global acquisition and development program, bringing its real estate expertise, collaborative processes, and tenant relationships to target markets in Mexico, Europe, and Asia.

At the end of 2002, AMB owned five facilities and more than 680,000 square feet in Guadalajara, Mexico; one facility with 786,979 square feet in Mexico City; and one facility and 67,415 square feet in Paris, France. The company is currently building in Singapore and looking for more opportunities in both Mexico and France.

"Our customers do not think of their business as domestic," Moghadam observes. "FedEx is global. Procter & Gamble is global. We have to be global to serve these clients in a consistent and seamless fashion."

AMB's global initiative is customer-driven in that it primarily addresses client space needs in foreign markets. The hardest part in the global process is finding the right partners, because the company invests only alongside partners in foreign countries. "The entrepreneurial and committed line partners are the ones that are hard to find, and that is where we spend most of our time," Moghadam says.

Relationships, patience, and forward thinking have been the hallmarks of Moghadam's success. He knows the product he is looking for and how it all fits in with his strategy. He refuses to be enticed into a deal on the allure of an existing structure and its tenants.

"A lot of people go along with a piece of real estate because it is very new or leased with credit tenants," he says. "High in-place rents are attractive to everyone, but it comes with a price, and you end up paying a lot for properties with those attributes." For instance, the credit quality of these tenants can change, or some new building more attractive than yours may be erected down the street.

Summarizing AMB's success, Moghadam reflects: "We look at our business more strategically than most real estate companies do. Generally, real estate people tend to be deal-oriented. If there is a good deal, they do it. It doesn't matter whether it is aligned with their strategy or not. Over time, we have realized that being sharp from a strategic focus is really important in terms of making us an effective long-term investor."

THE MAVERICK APPROACH TO BEING IN ALIGNMENT

1. Align investments with your operating strategy.
2. Stay focused and involved in the process.
3. Have a goal in mind and know what it will realistically take to achieve it.
4. Become a specialist in one real estate type.
5. Look for geographic diversity in your real estate holdings.
6. Private capital is usually the optimal source of investment funding.
7. View government regulations as merely a hindrance, not an obstacle.
8. Understand that a good reputation goes a long way.
9. When possible, build in areas that are strategically and financially beneficial to your customers.
10. Exercise patience in the pursuit of a great location.
11. Seek repeat business from your top customers.

CHAPTER 6

Find a Nearly Perfect Location

It's true that location is a critical factor in real estate investing. However, it is only a starting point. A good location won't necessarily save a bad investment, nor will a bad location prevent you from making money.

In one of many acquisitions over the years, Developers Diversified Realty (DDR), a Cleveland-based shopping center REIT, purchased a 560,000-square-foot retail center for $113.5 million in 2003. The attraction of the shopping center for DDR, as for so many of its other property acquisitions, was the location. It was in the heart of Pasadena, California's chichi retail district.

While the tenant mix was proportionately upscale—with stores by Tommy Bahama, Max Studio, Coach, J. Jill, and Ann Taylor Loft, among others—the key selling point was its location: in the center of a community with an average household income of $136,000, more than double the national average. Pasadena's median home value of $550,000 was also among the nation's highest.

All developers and acquirers of real estate cart out the old cliché of "location, location, location" to support their ventures, but what exactly does this mean? Truth is, for every real estate sector it means something different. The corner of two major thoroughfares works well for a shopping center, but not necessarily for a single-family residential development. New multifamily units can work in some dense urban locations while failing in others.

Something else to keep in mind is that a good location is not a constant. A tour of any large city demonstrates the phenomenon that the best location for an office building migrates over time. Even over the course of a decade, a regional mall can go from the best in market to the worst, as newer surrounding developments steal away foot traffic.

The Sherman Oaks Galleria mall in Los Angeles was once so trendy in regard to teenage fashion and behavior that it was featured in such movies as *Valley Girl* and *Fast Times at Ridgemont High*, quintessential teen movies from the early 1980s. Like a bad fashion statement, the Sherman Oaks Galleria succumbed to an outdated concept. By the end of the next decade, it was declared dead, stripped of its stores, and rebuilt as an office-retail complex.

The mall did not move on, but its clientele did. It was a good location for a shopping mall one decade, better as a mixed-use project the next.

Obviously, the breezy words "location, location, location" have to mean something to someone. They did to Howard Samuel, a British magnate who created a company called Land Securities PLC, which went on to become the largest land company in the United Kingdom. Somewhere in his mighty career, Samuel, who later became Lord Samuel, uttered for the first time the three repetitive words that have come to define the response to the question, "What are the three most important factors in real estate?"

A GOOD LOCATION WILL NOT SAVE BAD MANAGEMENT

Leave it to Donald Trump to put the location factor in perspective. As he observes, "I've seen people that are not particularly capable lose money in good locations, and I have seen capable people make a lot of money in bad locations."

Trump derides the location factor as the most misunderstood concept in all of real estate. The words "location, location, location," he says, are usually uttered by people who do not know what they are talking about. "You don't necessarily need the best location," he proclaims. "What you need is the best deal."[1]

Trump candidly avers that while the first step is to find a good location, if the numbers are not there, and if the financials are not favorable, then making the investment work out will likely be akin to pushing a boulder uphill.

Assuming the financials are sound and a good location is chosen, you also need savvy management to bring in the best tenants—and to keep those tenants even when the competition decides to trespass on your market area, as it always does.

EVEN THE BEST LOCATION
HAS TO MAKE FINANCIAL SENSE

The mantra of location has become so overwhelming that novices sometimes sacrifice common sense when they wander upon a great site for a particular kind of real estate. Believing the most important part of any deal is location, they overpay for the land, the building, and the rights, or they overleverage or strike a deal that is unfavorable. Even before they walk onto a property as the new owner, they are already fighting a losing battle.

Again, Trump quickly cuts to the heart of the matter. Real money, he stresses, is not made in real estate by spending top dollar to buy the best location. "You can get killed doing that. What you should never do is pay too much, even if that means walking away from a very good site."[2]

Any good location also has to work structurally. Does it have good access? Does it have good drainage? Is it environmentally contaminated? Does it work for what you have in mind? The good location you have found may be excellent for a retail complex, but not so great for an office building. And, if you want to build retail space, can you get the configuration you need?

During the 1980s, in a number of urban locations that were densely developed, new owners would pay high asking prices for real estate with excellent frontage on main thoroughfares thinking they could make the property pay by packing more space onto that one- or two-acre site by going vertical. It didn't work. There wasn't enough parking for a two- or three-story building, and, most problematic, retailers didn't want the upper stories.

LOCATION IS JUST ONE FACTOR

When looking at a piece of real estate and trying to decide if it is a good location, it is best to step back and figure out what will be built on the site. If, for example, the land would be perfect for an industrial building, there are a whole set of parameters to consider. Is there an adequate workforce in the immediate area? If not, is there a good transportation network for the workforce to commute to the location? How much parking will zoning allow? These same kinds of questions have to be asked whether you are building multifamily, office, or retail structures. It always comes back to the same considerations: population, accessibility, zoning, and site dynamics.

For some urban planners, development revolves around such criteria as good location, mixed-use concept, mass-transportation proximity, nearby housing, workable design, and pedestrian accessibility.[3]

It is amazing how just one of these factors can turn a perfect location into a disaster.

Randolph Self Storage, an operator and owner of small storage facilities, found a property it liked in Randolph, Massachusetts, and decided to build a new self-storage warehouse. Everything about the location was perfect until the company went to city hall for approval of its plans. It turns out this section of the city was zoned commercial. Because of the size of the proposed project, the city said a parking lot for 620 cars would need to be built based on its formula for commercial structures.

A self-storage facility gets few outside visitors to the office (cars pull into the facility and park by the individual storage units). Such facilities generally have parking for a half dozen cars. Randolph Self Storage estimated it would need just seven outside parking spots. It argued the required number of parking spaces bore no resemblance to the needs of the business where vehicle traffic was sporadic. The city council would not budge on the parking issue, thus making Randolph Self Storage's plan untenable.[4]

"Everybody says the three most important things in real estate are location, location, location, but that is old thinking," notes Richard LeFrak, president of the Lefrak Organization. "The three most important things in real estate are timing, timing, timing. If you finance conservatively, the fundamentals are good, and you deliver good value into a market when it is starved for that type of product, then there will be demand."

Appraisers have a unique point of view, since they are the ones who determine a property's base value. After working with a number of REITs, one appraiser summed up the experience this way: "The REITs seek out premier properties, ones that will retain their tenants and premium rents over the long run. These properties are called 'investment grade properties,' distinguishing them from non-investment-grade properties. There is one variable that typically defines an investment grade from a non-investment-grade property and that is price."[5]

Then how is price determined? By the amount of supply in the market, the demand for the property, and the availability of tenants willing to pay good rents. Whether or not a property is in a good location, says one appraiser, is really determined by these other factors.[6]

A slightly different view was taken by a real estate fund manager who acquired real estate on behalf of REITs, pension funds, and other institutional investors. Referring to retail, the fund manager's comments, though uttered in the mid-1990s, could certainly apply elsewhere and at any time. "What we look for is a combination of location, which has become more important than ever, and the anchor tenants," explained Thomas Caputo, a principal with the RREEF Funds in New York. "The presence or absence of competition and whether there are barriers to entry for new projects are also important factors."[7]

A senior executive at CB Commercial Real Estate Group takes a compromise position, suggesting, "The problem is the majority of properties are not prime quality. Investors primarily want Class A and A+ properties. Those properties that are not well located or well anchored and lack visibility will continue to trade at declining values."[8]

IT IS POSSIBLE TO *CREATE* A GOOD LOCATION

There are numerous examples across the country of developers discovering a piece of virgin real estate, erecting a project of their choice, and then watching as the once lonely building creates a stimulus for vast new development over a period of time. Achieving an even more difficult objective, but doing it equally successfully, are the visionaries who take a chance on a faltering and decaying old city block by building a development that provides the impetus for the redevelopment of a whole neighborhood.

Donald Trump's first successful urban project came in the early 1970s. The Commodore Hotel in New York was in such decline— the brick facade was absolutely filthy and the lobby appallingly dingy—it looked like a welfare hotel. Surrounding the property were boarded-up storefronts.[9] The neighborhood was already run-down and not expected to get any better any time soon.

However, with the hotel's proximity to Grand Central Station, with millions of pedestrians passing the property, Trump intuitively realized that if he could create a dynamic, landmark hotel, then the neighborhood would follow in redevelopment, which is exactly what happened.

On the West Coast, Frank Lowy, chairman of Australia's Lend Lease Corporation, took a similar gamble with one of his first purchases in the United States. The site was a retail shopping center with a supermarket and half a dozen small shops. Although not very appealing, Lowy scouted the area and realized the site, sitting on the boundary between Beverly Hills and Santa Monica and surrounded by a high-income population of 500,000, was the epitome of a good location if it could be redeveloped.

Lowy's idea was to tear down the existing structures and build a multilevel center covering the entire space. The land was too valuable to waste on parking, which could be handled by underground and rooftop usage.

Before making the deal, Lowy needed to know whether the city's zoning would change if he tore down the existing structures. If he rebuilt, could he get approval for his parking concept? He asked for and received written approval from the city in advance. Westfield Pavilions then became the first shopping center in the United States with rooftop parking.[10]

Houston-based Hines is known today for its bold, well-designed skyscrapers, such as One Shell Plaza in Houston, Wells Fargo Center (originally United Bank Center) in Denver, 53rd At Third in New York, and the Tour EDF Tower in Paris's La Defense. In the company's early days, it took a risky gamble on some pastureland west of Houston.

There were indications that Houston's development was heading toward the west. As Gerald Hines, founder and chairman of Hines, recalls, the thought was that they would build retail, "but the land we bought was six times more expensive than where you would put normal retail."

His solution was to intensify the land use. He constructed a three-story shopping mall with an ice-skating rink on the bottom level and a health club on the rooftop. Hines eventually added an office building and hotel because, he says, "we needed to justify the cost we paid for the land."

The shopping center, known as The Galleria, became one of the most storied and copied regional shopping malls in the United States. The area surrounding The Galleria is now a densely built-up section of Houston, with office buildings, hotels, and residential structures all surrounding the shopping center, which has undergone three large additions over the years. (Hines sold the property in 1999.)

RELY ON THE FUNDAMENTALS

You can create a location, but you must have basic fundamentals going for the property, opines Jeffrey Hines, Gerald Hines's son and the company's president. "There are a lot of elements at work here. It depends on where you think your customers will be coming from and where your tenants are now. Sometimes you can get a secondary location, and if it turns out well, you can send a city's development patterns in a whole new direction."

Ultimately, Hines develops on well-located sites, but the end development has some bearing on whether the site will prove to be a great location, according to Gerald Hines.

"Our firm," adds Jeffrey Hines, "spends a lot of time looking at the demand statistics of various submarkets."

A GOOD LOCATION MAY NOT STAY THAT WAY

Location is a dynamic concept, suggests Jeffrey Hines, meaning that what happens to the surrounding neighborhood, the region, and perhaps even the state economically and socially can reduce a once good location to a tertiary market.

Location is not static, but you can do things to try to keep the property in good condition for a long time. Hines's corporate theory is to create quality buildings that people will want to stay in through up and down cycles.

"We cannot control rental rates, but we can try to control occupancy rates," says Jeffrey Hines. "We want to reduce occupancy risk as much as possible, and the way to do that is to rent to the upper end of the spectrum."

To Hines's way of thinking, if you build low-quality structures, you will attract low-quality tenants. At the first hint of economic trouble these tenants will slink away in the middle of the night.

"It's important to understand," says Jeffrey Hines, "that you can mess up a good location."

BE DILIGENT AND WAIT FOR OPPORTUNITIES

Born in 1925, Gerald Hines was raised in Gary, Indiana. He proudly extended his Indiana education by attending Purdue University, where he earned a degree in mechanical engineering. His first important job after college and a stint in the armed services was as an engineer with a company that built and supplied air-conditioning equipment for large office buildings. The company gave him three options of cities in which to work. Hines chose Houston, a city he had never before seen.

In 1952, while still working on air-conditioning and mechanical systems for office buildings, Gerald Hines was talking with a neighbor who mentioned he needed a warehouse for his business. Hines said he could build it for him, and he did—all 5,000 square feet.

Gerald Hines enjoyed the work so much he continued to build small warehouses while holding down his job as an engineer. In 1957, guessing he could support his family by doing commercial construction, Hines quit his day job and opened a small office in downtown Houston.

In the 1950s, Houston was expanding rapidly. Indeed, Gerald Hines had guessed right. There was a lot of work even for a small

MEET THE MAVERICKS

Gerald Hines

Birth Date: 1925

Occupation: Founder and Chairman, Hines, Houston, TX

Education: BS, mechanical engineering, Purdue University; honorary doctorate of engineering, Purdue University

Career Highlights:
- Creates Hines, a Houston real estate development and management company
- Develops The Galleria shopping mall and tops off One Shell Plaza in Houston
- Develops the 75-story, I. M. Pei–designed J.P. Morgan Chase Tower (was Texas Commerce Tower) in Houston
- Develops oval-shaped 53rd At Third in New York
- University of Houston renames school of architecture The Gerald D. Hines School of Architecture

company. Within two years, Gerald Hines's little firm had constructed eight buildings, and a portfolio of properties began to form.

As the go-go 1960s rolled in, Gerald Hines was suddenly a very busy man. By 1967, a decade after opening his own shop, his company constructed 97 warehouse, office, retail, parking, and residential structures. Suddenly, Hines controlled a lot of Houston real estate.

It was time for Gerald Hines to move to bigger things. In 1970, phase one of The Galleria in Houston opened. Modeled after Milan's Galleria Vittorio Emanuelle, it was a harbinger of the large, upscale malls that would dot America over the next 30 years. One year later, Hines topped off its first office tower, the 50-story One Shell Plaza in Houston, which at the time was the largest reinforced concrete structure in the world.

One Shell Plaza marked a turning point for the firm. For the design of the building, Gerald Hines hired Bruce Graham, one of the leading architects of high-rise buildings. Going forward, Hines would always opt for high-quality structures designed by the best in the world, most notably Philip Johnson, who designed 13 different projects for Hines, including five in Houston. Johnson also designed the rounded, pink-hued 53rd At Third in New York, which is often referred to as the "lipstick building." Other architects who have worked with Hines include Sir Norman Foster, Frank Gehry, I. M. Pei, and Cesar Pelli.

Another attention-getter is Houston's Philip Johnson–designed Pennzoil Place, where the two towers are separated by a sliver of sky that appears to split a single building in two.[11]

HIGH QUALITY AND STABLE FINANCING
CREATE A GOOD LOCATION

Gerald Hines eventually developed a three-pronged mantra by which he operated: Spend extra dollars on centrally located sites, use brand-name architects, and offer first-class amenities.

Tenants, Gerald Hines says, "like to feel that heavy hardware. Just like a good Mercedes or Lincoln door, when you slam it, it sounds good." When times are good, those expensive details can translate into higher rents, but more important, when times are bad, as they were during the Houston oil bust of the mid-1980s, they keep the tenants.[12]

"In a soft market, tenants are going to go to the highest-quality space," adds Jeffrey Hines.[13]

When a cycle turns, the poorer-quality buildings lose tenants to higher-quality buildings, with the latter continually maintaining the essential qualities of a good location. Half-empty office buildings will not turn a prosperous neighborhood into a problem area, but they will strand development in that particular area until the economy comes back.

"We did not see the real estate recession of the late 1980s coming any more than anyone else did," notes Jeffrey Hines. "But we had an absolute belief that real estate is cyclical, so we had a conservative financial structure put in place as a long-term strategy."

It turned out to be a good thing, because the Hines firm was very portfolio heavy in Houston, and that market turned ugly way before other cities. "We saw the demand/supply imbalance was coming and we started dropping our rates faster than the market. We wanted to fill up our buildings quickly, and we used that same strategy across the country," says Jeffrey Hines.

It is not enough just to maintain the mantra of site, architecture, and amenities; Hines learned early on that financing can just as easily make or break you.

The Galleria and One Shell Plaza were almost bet-the-ranch types of projects. Failure with either could have been the end of the line for the company. Gerald Hines clearly admits he did not sleep well during the months those projects were in development.

"The original financings on the two projects were the standard developer's strategy of the time, that is, let's leverage this as much as we can," explains Jeffrey Hines. "After The Galleria and One Shell Plaza, the company began to change. We had learned our lesson early. In the 1970s and 1980s, when everyone else was still putting on as much leverage as possible, we were doing buildings with almost zero debt. Our financing strategies are much more conservative."

In 1990, Gerald Hines moved up from operations to company chairman and Jeffrey Hines became president and then chief executive. The two Hineses, father and son, tend to champion each other's merits in conversation, but physically and in regard to corporate decisions, they are dissimilar. The older Hines, who continues to work hard for the company he founded by directing European operations from London, is of slight build. Considered a natty dresser, he is distinguished in appearance and careful in spoken word.

Jeffrey Hines is a much larger man, with the round face of a cheery blue-collar Joe. He looks and talks busy, with sentences and phrases that rush from his mouth.

In a world of hard-charging, often brusque real estate mavens, the two Hineses are about as pleasant and polite as two gentlemen can be.

If Gerald Hines was a gambler early in his real estate career, he quickly moved to become a visionary in design and architecture. The son makes no claims to aesthetics and as CEO has refined the financial conservatism that the elder Hines began in prior decades. It is said the younger Hines has been more focused on expanding the Hines empire, while keeping its essential conservative financial structure intact.[14]

Jeffrey Hines, born in 1955, was raised in Houston. After graduating from high school, he headed north to Williams College in Massachusetts, where he earned a degree in economics. After working at a bank in Houston, he returned to Massachusetts and received his MBA from Harvard Business School.

One of his first jobs after joining his father's company was being on-site at the construction of what is now the Bank of America building in downtown Houston. After eight years of working his way through the ranks, he became president of the company.

MEET THE MAVERICKS

Jeffrey Hines

Birth Date: 1955

Occupation: President and Chief Executive, Hines, Houston, TX

Education: BA, economics, Williams College; MBA, Harvard Graduate School of Business

Career Highlights:

- Instrumental in the creation and development of the firm's $846 million Emerging Markets Fund
- Develops 56-story Philip Johnson and John Burgee–designed Bank of America Center in Houston
- Develops the firm's domestic and international acquisition program, which has been responsible for initiating acquisitions totaling in excess of $2.5 billion
- Oversees entry into the China markets; projects include Embassy House and Park Avenue high-rise residential developments in Beijing
- Boosts third-party construction business, including developments for large financial institutions

With his seat-of-the-pants development of The Galleria and One Shell Plaza behind him, Gerald Hines moved to equity investing, rather than borrowing. He recruited institutional investors such as pension funds, and even received an infusion from the investment office of Kuwait. The firm puts its own capital into projects, usually up to 30 percent, plus it earns management fees and an additional

20 percent of the profit when there is a sale. The Hineses like to hold onto their properties.[15]

Jeffrey Hines refined the art of capital raising. "Over the last five to six years, we have moved from financing on a one-off basis, where we put together a deal and go find an investor for the particular project, to programmatic investing," he explains. In essence, Hines derived a real estate strategy involving multiple projects and raises capital in advance, usually in the form of investment funds.

Hines, together with Trust Company of the West Group and the old Dean Witter Realty, formed a $410 million fund in 1996 to invest in emerging markets. The company also has financing partnerships with the California Public Employees' Retirement System and General Motors Asset Management.[16]

Jeffrey Hines currently runs a privately owned real estate firm that is one of the largest in the world. It continues to be involved in developing, acquiring, leasing, and managing, as well as providing global investment management and advisory services. Its portfolio totals 700 properties, representing 223 million square feet of office, mixed-use, industrial, hotel, sports, and residential properties, plus large, master-planned communities. With offices in 74 U.S. cities and 11 foreign countries, Hines controls assets valued in excess of $13 billion.

"We are a matrix organization," says Jeffrey Hines. "We are organized geographically, six regions in the United States and Europe. Other international locations fall under the reach of domestic organizations. For example, the Far East falls under the structure of our West Region group."

Each regional division consists of a development manager, project manager, accountants, property managers, and executives, whom Hines likes to think of as the top resources that can be given to bear on any situation. The company uses a central construction group that gets involved in the early stages of design, contract bidding, engineering, and interfacing with architects. There is also a central finance group.

SOMETIMES THE BEST SITES ARE OVERSEAS

Despite being almost 80, Gerald Hines can still be found frequently in his company's London office directing European operations, which have become quite extensive. The company's projects spread from France to Russia and Poland to Spain.

The firm has moved slowly into international markets, with projects in Mexico and Canada. In the early 1990s, it made a conscious decision to be in Europe. The event that probably changed the Hineses' collective minds about Europe was the fall of the Berlin Wall in 1991. The company very quickly erected two major projects in the reunified city. It has also built the Frank Gehry–designed DG Bank headquarters near the Brandenburg Gate.[17]

"We just felt there was more opportunity and a greater playing field in Berlin," says Gerald Hines. "Berlin and then Moscow worked out so well, we started to move gently from one country to another. From Germany we went to France and then Spain and Italy."

The company was careful at first in regard to international expansion, which gave management time to explore various possibilities in different cities, especially those places where U.S. clients were looking to expand. "We were getting a lot of responses from tenants that were becoming global companies and not finding the sort of office product they wanted," says Gerald Hines. "They were begging for a Hines-quality project, and also our investors were looking to diversify their real estate portfolio. So, we were getting some pushes to go international."

In 1997, Hines began construction on a $600 million project called Diagonal Mar in Barcelona, a huge complex of buildings on 85 acres along the Mediterranean Sea. It was, at the time, Hines's largest undertaking in Europe and probably biggest project on the continent. The first buildings completed were for a large shopping center. By 2003, the residential development was 70 percent finished, but there were still build-outs to do on a convention center and office towers.

When Hines began growing its operations in Europe, it benefited from high rental rates in the major cities, little or no competition, and some very good deals. For example, the land in Barcelona was originally owned by Kemper Insurance out of Chicago, which had put $400 million into it. "We bought it for $10 million, plus a $5 million note," says Jeffrey Hines. "That was a pretty good write-down."

In 1999 alone, Hines completed the Mala Sarka residential development in Prague, the Pariser Platz 3 office and residential development in Berlin, and the Main Tower in Frankfurt.

In 2001 and 2002, about 50 percent of the company's projects were outside the United States.[18]

"There was a fair amount of risk going to Europe," says Jeffrey Hines. "We now have a large organization over there. We have the capital to make deals, and we are still following the leads of the people we have on the ground. We have now passed the risk stage."

EVERY BUILDING IS A SEPARATE STORY

As the company gets larger and its portfolio of properties gets bigger and bigger, it is still important to look at each investment on a building-by-building basis.

As Jeffrey Hines explains, "Each building is sort of a separate business." The advantage of a large company is that it has the organizational structure and financial resources to find the people to run those separate businesses.

"We try not to get too corporate. We bring people from the field into a lot of the decision making," Jeffrey Hines continues. "We think it is important to have a flat structure, where they can call me or my father and get information in minutes rather than go through the organizational chain."

Jeffrey Hines concedes there are some advantages to becoming a public company, such as access to capital, but Hines has managed to do well despite the lack of access to public markets. "When we have found good projects, we have been able to find capital," says Jeffrey Hines. "And we have done quite well by our investors."

The trade-off in remaining a private, family-run company is flexibility.

"The reason we never went public," says Jeffrey Hines, "is that we believe real estate is a long-term business. It cannot be run by managing on a quarterly earnings statement basis. We could never have become international as a public company, because it is a long-term investment. It was very difficult, very expensive, and it took a lot of organizational resources. If we were a public company, we wouldn't be able to justify the move."

ADAPT AND CHANGE

Over the years, the company has changed in many ways. Hines had always believed in holding onto its real estate. During the real estate recession years of the late 1980s and early 1990s, it did sell some buildings, but it really wasn't the corporate philosophy.

In the 1990s, as the firm began to use investment funds more and more to develop projects, it necessitated a change to its long-standing develop-and-hold strategy. "We have done a couple of funds where we have adopted a merchant building strategy, that is, to operate the building for a number of years, then sell," says Jeffrey Hines. "We raised a fund around that strategy and it has been a real success. These funds have defined lives, so we have to sell, and we are always looking for the right time. Selling has become much more a part of the equation than it was in the 1980s, that's for sure."

The company has changed in other ways as well. After the real estate recession years that stretched into the 1990s, Hines began doing more third-party development. "After the market turned in the 1980s, it was clear we had to make some changes," Jeffrey Hines says. "It wasn't possible to just be a developer in the traditional sense anymore."[19]

Throughout the 1990s, Hines took on an increasing number of high-profile, third-party businesses, including a $500 million redevelopment of the Renaissance Center in Detroit, the headquarters buildings for Morgan Stanley in midtown Manhattan, the Audrey Jones Beck Building of the Museum of Fine Arts in Houston, and the Boston Red Sox spring training ballpark in Fort Myers, Florida.

The thing that has not changed over the almost five decades since Hines was formed is a belief in, not location, location, location, but local, local, local—that real estate is a local business and decisions need to be made locally.

"There is no magic formula for success," Jeffrey Hines adds. "While we pay attention to national statistics, in the end we usually default to our person who is in the market and lives and breathes that market, who understands that two street corners 100 yards apart can be completely different submarkets. That is usually who we pay most attention to in our decision-making process."

THE MAVERICK APPROACH TO FINDING A NEARLY PERFECT LOCATION

1. A good location today might not stay that way forever.
2. A good location alone is no substitute for bad management.
3. Even the best location has to work out financially and structurally. In other words, if you don't get a good deal on the price, location alone probably will not save you.
4. Despite what you may have heard, location is really just one factor to consider.
5. An equally important factor is *timing.*
6. It is possible to create a good location if the fundamentals are in your favor.
7. If you are diligent, opportunities in good locations will come to you.
8. High-quality structures and stable financing can help to create a good location.
9. Sometimes the best locations are overseas.
10. Be sure to check local zoning requirements to confirm that your property is welcome at the site.
11. Remember, a good location for an office isn't necessarily the best location for a warehouse or a residential development. Good locations must be relevant to your project.

CHAPTER 7

Benefit from Someone Else's Disasters

One person's investment failure
can become a Maverick's gold mine.
Distressed real estate is the basic
foodstuff of opportunistic investors. But
distress comes in various forms, from
physical deterioration to financial disaster.
As a result, it still takes a good eye to
spot gold nuggets in the hard dirt.

When building company Al Neyer Inc. was hired to construct an industrial plant in Blue Ash, a suburban Cincinnati community, the land was still fairly undeveloped. It was the early 1970s, and the new building was to become home to a check-printing company.

Thirty years later, Cincinnati-based Al Neyer was looking for some development land and stumbled upon a vacant industrial site—the old check-printing plant it had erected years before. Buying the land for $2.3 million, it razed the structure and constructed a five-story, 132,000-square-foot office building. In a short period of time, the new building was 100 percent leased, with the lead tenant, Sara Lee Corporation, choosing to house a corporate division there. The value of the new project jumped to $20 million.[1]

Many of the best-known real estate projects were pioneering developments erected on land that, though pristine, was merely at the cusp of a population surge. Other projects were lonely outputs that eventually attracted a wave of city-building. Equally as adventuresome are the investors and developers who recognize value in urban wastelands, nearly deserted developments, or in new buildings that proved financially catastrophic to the original owners.

CO-INVESTMENT IS ALWAYS A GOOD OPTION

In the late 1980s, when developers were going bust at a record pace, smart investors quickly realized a killing could be made by raising capital and buying offices, hotels, shopping centers, and business parks for dimes on the dollar. A whole new category of investment vehicle, the *vulture fund,* evolved just for these purposes. The idea was to create a limited partnership that would invest in depressed property with the goal of profiting when prices rebounded.[2]

The vulture fund eventually gave way to a more formal investment vehicle carrying the politically correct investment appellation
opportunity fund. The concept of the opportunity fund was simple:
When real estate markets softened, investment firms would form
private equity real estate funds (essentially pools of capital from
investors) to seek out acquisition opportunities. These funds would
purchase underperforming and even distressed real estate to reposi-
tion the properties. The goal was to produce annual returns in the
10 percent range, but during the 1990s, returns of 20 percent or better were not unusual.

Opportunity funds were generally organized by big investment
banks such as Goldman Sachs, but smaller groups could and did
start similar programs. As always, the thinking behind these funds
is that when you create a pool of capital, the dollars are there and
available for any opportunities that suddenly arise. In addition,
pools of capital can be leveraged, meaning more or bigger deals can
be transacted.

FIND THE TRUE LAND VALUE

Distressed is an adjective tossed around a lot by real estate investors.
Opportunity funds certainly targeted those developments that were
physically distressed yet had appealing qualities—most important,
strategic locations.

Not all distressed properties can be saved. Even if the building
itself cannot be renovated, a distressed project in an area where there
is inherent value for future growth holds land value. Obviously, certain expensive risks are involved, not the least of which can be environmentally compromised ground that needs to be cleaned up. Still,
if the demographic trendline is there, it could be worth taking the
gamble.

Al Neyer did not really take such a gamble. The company just had a sharp eye for a deal. The Blue Ash neighborhood where the old printing plant once stood was within the loop of the city's main traffic arteries and within a short commuting distance of Cincinnati's downtown. Extensive redevelopment had already been going on.

FIGURE OUT THE REPLACEMENT COST

At the end of the 1980s, when the real estate markets began to tank big-time, Maverick Sam Zell noticed a lot of Class A (high-rise) property was being tossed back into the market by desperate owners who were heavily leveraged. One might say he smelled opportunity. Acting on his keen senses, Zell borrowed heavily to buy up buildings at bargain prices.[3]

It wasn't so much that buildings could be bought cheaply, but that Zell realized they could be bought *below* their replacement cost. This became his guideline for future deals. "Philosophically, one of Zell's things was that the key to real estate was understanding replacement costs, then on top of that, understanding your competitor's cost to come into your market and compete against you," explains Jay Leupp, a managing director with RBC Capital Markets. "That is why he was so active in the early 1990s, because he could buy real estate below replacement cost."

This is an easy concept to understand. It is simply being able to acquire a property at or below the cost of developing that property at today's cost structure. Unfortunately, it is not always easy to find such buildings.

The late 1980s and early 1990s were extremely unique times. During the previous decade, capital for building was so liquid, development far outstripped the demand for such properties. When the economy began to slow, the real estate industry and then lenders entered into extremely rough waters—so much so that the savings and loan industry, which handed out massive amounts of money to real estate buyers before the bubble burst, almost succumbed.

GET THE COMPETITIVE ADVANTAGE

Zell's twist on replacement cost, which he put into practice in the late 1980s, involved two things: (1) buying property at or below the cost of developing a similar property and (2) having a price so low he could retain a competitive advantage over whomever might build the next great thing across the street.

It also helps if a barrier to entry makes it difficult for others to do what you are doing.

"Let's talk about how you make money," Zell offers. "Has anybody ever made money without a barrier to entry from competitors? The laws of economics haven't been reversed. It's all about supply and demand, barriers to entry, execution market share . . . and earnings."[4]

Class A buildings continued to come back onto the market through the mid-1990s, before the stream petered out. Another recession at the beginning of the new millennium did not have the same effect as the one a decade earlier. Due to the low interest rate environment, most owners could refinance instead of having to unload properties.

The pursuit of buildings that could be bought at or below replacement cost is a worthwhile goal of opportunistic investors. As one real estate investment company noted, "Our objective is to purchase quality multifamily communities in temporarily distressed growth markets at prices below replacement costs." The same company also declared that each community it develops is thoroughly scrutinized to create a plan for enhancing operations and cash flow.[5]

That is really the secret to buying below replacement cost buildings.

It's not enough to find the deals. As an investor, you must implement a program to manage that building successfully, build tenant occupancy, stabilize rents, and improve cash flow.

Chicago-based Transwestern Commercial Services boasts a formalized approach. The company looks for assets that have the potential to appeal to institutional investors, but that come on the market with significant lease risk, have been mismanaged, need repositioning, or require significant capital expenditures. In addition, Transwestern focuses on properties that have some value-added component. The goal then becomes the execution of a business plan and delivering a stabilized institutional quality asset to core buyers with a lower cost of capital. While budgeting its capital expenditures, Transwestern pays specific attention to cost-benefit analysis and the payback period.[6]

In December 2002, New Boston Fund, a real estate development and investment firm, announced the sale of a 142,000-square-foot office building in Windsor, Connecticut. The price was $12.35 million. Six years earlier, New Boston had bought the building for $8.2 million.

According to the company, the building was initially acquired at 44 percent of replacement cost, making it an "attractive investment from the beginning." The sale generated a profit of more than 100 percent on New Boston's equity. To rub it in a little more, the company bragged, its investors realized sizable returns at a time when alternative investments such as the stock market had experienced sizable losses.[7]

LOOK FOR REUSE POTENTIAL

Many of the buildings scooped up by Zell and other opportunistic investors in the period from the late 1980s to mid-1990s were restored to financial health by bringing in capital and/or new management. They were then either added to portfolios or turned around and sold for profit. Distressed high-rise offices became healthy office buildings; weak multifamily properties were turned into near-full-occupancy projects; and struggling hotels got polished and rebranded.

The outcome was always in sight for those properties that just needed a helping hand and good oversight. The real diamonds in the rough are the extremely distressed properties that look hopeless. Some of these structures should be torn down and, as noted, considered solely for the value of the land. Creative developers sometimes see totally new uses for older buildings. Downtown Los Angeles has recently experienced a population in-migration due to the creative reuse of older and sometimes abandoned office and industrial buildings.

It is hard to say what Tom Aderhold, president of Aderhold Properties in Atlanta, thought when he first stood in front of the old Fulton Cotton Mill in Atlanta. This huge complex was spread out over nine abandoned buildings. He undoubtedly had a stream of creative consciousness, because Aderhold Properties bought the old mill property and transformed it into a 505-unit apartment community.

The oldest building in the complex, built in 1881, could not be rehabilitated, so Aderhold Properties kept the walls, which now surround the swimming pool. "It has the look of an old Roman ruin," says Aderhold.[8]

Creative reuse, if successful, can start unintentional trendiness, with other developers rushing in where pioneers once trod. In the best-case scenario, derelict neigborhoods such as Tribeca in New York City become hot spots. For developers, the real chance to cash in is at the beginning, because once unintentional trendiness begins, prices escalate significantly.

FINANCIAL DISTRESS IS BETTER
THAN PROPERTY DISTRESS

The deal that transformed Canadian megadeveloper Olympia & York from a small, regional company into a development powerhouse came about through the financial distress of 1960s megadeveloper William Zeckendorf.

Until the rise of Olympia & York, Zeckendorf, through his company Webb & Knapp, was probably the most daring dealer in real property in United States history. He built Century City in Los Angeles, Mile High Center in Denver, L'Enfant Plaza in Washington, D.C., and numerous other gargantuan developments.[9]

Zeckendorf was sitting on a huge development just outside of Toronto called Flemingdon Park. The 400-plus-acre project was in midconstruction when Zeckendorf ran into serious financial problems. In 1963, Zeckendorf began dangling the project before scores of developers in Canada and the United States. As one Webb & Knapp executive noted, "The real estate community saw us reaching the bottom of the barrel and thought whatever was left must not be very good apples. In reality, there was nothing wrong with Flemingdon Park that cash couldn't cure."[10]

One person who saw the value of the project was Paul Reichmann, who controlled Olympia & York, along with his brother, Albert Reichmann. Paul Reichmann organized a joint venture with investors to buy a 50 percent interest in Flemingdon Park for $18 million. Eventually Zeckendorf's problem was transformed into the largest suburban office park in Canada. "Flemingdon Park would prove every bit the bonanza that Paul Reichmann had envisioned."[11]

In some regard, the deal and subsequent development launched the relatively unknown Reichmanns into the next level of real estate prominence in Canada and then elsewhere around the world.

Generally, when one hears the word *distressed* in reference to a property, the initial thought is that the land or buildings are somehow compromised or derelict. In fact, many good deals occur when a property stands in satisfactory condition, but its owners are in financial disarray, or the capital underpinnings of the transaction that either created the property or acquired it have become burdensome.

To go after a property where there is financial distress is always tricky. Although the owners want to get out, they generally have certain requirements they want fulfilled. Occasionally, one comes across an owner in desperate condition who will give in to any proposal, but that is rare. Most often, one finds an owner who is trying to get out from under a possibly distressed loan situation, but who is not willing to give the property away.

In such cases, there undoubtedly will be other investors competing for those assets.

ASCERTAIN THE SELLER'S BASIC REQUIREMENTS

Good opportunistic buyers take the time to figure out what the seller wants, guessing the kind of terms the seller is seeking and an approximation of the selling point. In addition, opportunistic buyers scrutinize the properties in question, because even in financially distressed situations, there will be reinvestment. The final cost almost always is much more than the settled price of the deal.

Distress sellers have an obvious weakness that should be exploited.

If the buyer's strategy is to buy, renovate, and sell, the opportunistic deal maker has to get a sense of the hold time. Properties cannot be tossed back into the market during a down cycle.

The Bernstein Companies of Washington, D.C., formed Consortium Capital, which consists of a series of limited partnership funds that raise capital to invest in opportunistic commercial real estate plays in the Mid-Atlantic region. The funds typically partner with a buyer who has taken out a first mortgage. Consortium then provides the rest of the financing to make the deal work. It can do its own deals or provide 100 percent of the equity necessary to complete an acquisition. Equity funding provided by Consortium then can be used to guarantee debt, buy out partners, finance speculative development or redevelopment, or even solve tax problems.

When the Reichmann's Olympia & York moved into Manhattan, it did so by purchasing a portfolio of properties in a transaction so lucrative it is still considered to be one of the company's best real estate deals, perhaps even better than Flemingdon Park. Putting his name on the dotted line secured for Paul Reichmann eight skyscrapers that a financially distressed National Kinney Corporation was desperate to sell.

Although a number of Maverick real estate investors, including Sam LeFrak, had looked at the properties and made bids, Reichmann managed to purchase the portfolio for $46 million. Within a decade, the value of the buildings rose to $3 billion.[12]

It was not that the buildings were distressed, although they needed millions of dollars in investment for renovation and rehabilitation. Rather, there was a recession in the country and New York property owners were getting hit very hard.

About the time the Reichmanns were shopping in Manhattan, Sam Zell, a Chicago investor, wrote an article in a real estate trade publication, noting, "The opportunity of acquiring real estate in its current distress offers the greatest single economic opportunity for investors in our time."[13]

Zell would later do a deal or two with the Reichmanns. More important, his observations about buying in the throes of a recession proved correct, as the value of properties immediately began to climb again when the economy stabilized. A decade later, he put the lesson learned in the late 1970s recession to good use.

BANKS CAN HELP YOU AND HELP THEMSELVES

Until the 1980s, real estate had been a highly fragmented, locally based industry financed for the most part by savings and loans, banks, and, to a lesser extent (for bigger projects), insurance companies. Wall Street or some other investment banking entity would occasionally also step in to raise capital for a major development.

When the United States entered into a severe real estate depression, induced partly by the elimination of key tax incentives to the industry, highly leveraged borrowers could no longer repay loans. Defaults collapsed numerous financial institutions, most notably the thrifts.[14]

Zell, who a decade before had hypothesized about opportunities available in down cycles, swung into action so effectively that he became known as the "grave dancer."

"He made a name for himself as the grave dancer by buying distressed properties from banks that had foreclosed on them, as well as developers that were in trouble," Leupp observes. "In many cases, he was able to get low-cost leverage from banks that wanted real estate off their balance sheets. He would bid very low prices, obtain financing, often from the institutions that wanted to be rid of the real estate they had taken back from developers."

Zell borrowed heavily and bought up scores of properties at bargain prices.[15] He very quickly became one of the largest investors in real estate during the downturn in the late 1980s and early 1990s, adds Rod Petrik, a managing director with Legg Mason Wood Walker. "There was blood on the streets and Zell was one of the first and certainly one of the largest investors in buying real estate in that down cycle."

MEET THE MAVERICKS

Samuel Zell

Birth Date: 1942

Occupation: Chairman of Equity Residential, Chairman of
Equity Office Properties Trust, Chairman of
Manufactured Homes Communities, all in
Chicago, IL

Education: BA, political science, University of Michigan; JD,
University of Michigan Law School

Career Highlights:

- Moves to Chicago and begins to syndicate real estate deals
- Creates pioneering opportunity funds to buy distressed properties during late 1980s and early 1990s real estate recession
- Creates Equity Residential, the largest apartment REIT in the country
- Creates Equity Office Properties, the largest REIT in the United States
- Creates Manufactured Home Communities to aggregate properties in that sector

FIND WILLING INVESTORS

Zell realized he did not have the fortune available to take advantage of all the deals suddenly appearing in the marketplace, so he created an investment vehicle for those who would trust his judgment.

As the steam began to leak out of the booming 1980s real estate cycle, Zell astutely visualized the continuum of events that was beginning to unfold. The excessive leveraging of properties could not continue, he surmised. Lenders would be forced to foreclose, and then they would need to unload these distressed properties to reduce their real estate loan exposure. To amass a war chest for such deals, Zell joined forces with Wall Street and formed Zell-Merrill I, a pioneering opportunity fund that raised what seemed at the time to be a huge amount of capital—$409 million.[16]

As the decade of the 1990s rolled in, lenders were foreclosing on properties at a frantic pace. Finally, the federal government stepped in, accumulating vast pools of nonperforming real estate loans in the foreclosure of insolvent financial institutions via the Resolution Trust Corporation. Zell-Merrill I was often the only potential buyer for the RTC's high-quality properties.[17]

When *Realtor* magazine listed the most influential people in real estate in 2000, it said of Zell, "With key partners, Zell cobbled together huge investment funds in the 1980s that enabled him to control one of the largest office and apartment portfolios in the country. And he did it in the way that other investors dream about: by taking undervalued properties off the hands of financially distressed owners—in other words by buying low."[18]

IT'S WHAT YOU DO NEXT THAT'S IMPORTANT

There are two theories about what happened next with the empire Zell cobbled together in the late 1980s and early 1990s. The positive picture is that when the economy took off in the 1990s, Zell was not just in fat city—he owned it.[19]

While that may be true, another thought is that in the early 1990s, Zell had a lot of debt coming due. It also was a time (1990) when Zell's longtime partner, Bob Lurie, died of cancer. Lurie generally oversaw the business operations.

Zell reorganized his holdings into a pair of public companies, which eventually became the two largest REITs in the country: Equity Residential went public in 1994, and Equity Office Properties Trust came to market in 1997. Zell also chairs a third REIT, Manufactured Home Communities. All are based in Chicago.

Zell was a deal maker, while Bob Lurie was a numbers guy. They had worked together since meeting in college. "Sam wasn't about to sit in the back room and run the numbers," recalls Ann Lurie, Bob's wife, "and Bob was not about to go all over the country doing the backslapping and deal making." In short, Lurie handled the organization and books; Zell scouted and cut the deals.[20]

After Lurie died, it made sense to change the organizational structure of his businesses and bring in good operational people, which is what he did immediately with Equity Residential. Zell hired Douglas Crocker in 1992 and let him put his stamp on the company. (Crocker retired in 2002.)

"Since Equity Residential went public, the bulk of its success has got a lot to do with Crocker," says Petrik. "Sam recognized that he had a very capable CEO and gave him free rein. He knew to get the hell out of the way, and that he didn't need to get involved in the day-to-day of the company. That was Doug Crocker's job."

When Equity Residential went public, Petrik adds, it had a market capitalization of about $400 million. Now its market cap is $7.5 billion.

Equity Residential was formed a year before it went public, in March 1993. Today it is engaged in the acquisition, ownership, management, and operation of multifamily properties. With more than 1,000 properties across 36 states, it is the largest publicly owned operator of apartment communities in the United States. As of the latest numbers, it has full ownership of 906 properties and 191,875 units, partial ownership (consolidated) of 36 properties and 6,931 units, and unconsolidated ownership of 85 properties and 22,443 units.

Equity Residential, based on market capitalization, is the second largest U.S.-based REIT, after Equity Office Properties, which is the largest publicly held owner of office properties in the country. The company manages 125.5 million square feet of primarily Class A office space in 729 buildings in 32 major metropolitan areas.

Equity Office, the first real estate company to be named to the Standard and Poor's 500 Index, traces its origins back to 1976, when Zell founded an integrated real estate management and acquisition organization. Since its public offering, the company has nearly quadrupled in size through mergers and acquisitions. Its biggest deals were the $4.3 billion Beacon Properties merger in December 1997, the $4.5 billion Cornerstone Properties merger in June 2000, and the $7.2 billion Spieker Properties merger in July 2001.

The Beacon deal was typical of Zell's thinking and led the way for the subsequent mergers. The aim, Zell said at the time, was to give "Equity a dominant position in Boston, the one major market in which the company lagged behind the competition." The concept of buying to be big in a single major market worked well until the Spieker Properties deal in July 2001. Spieker was strong in northern California, especially in cities like San Jose and San Francisco, where Equity didn't have a large presence. Touted as the largest REIT deal ever, the Spieker Properties transaction was also one of Zell's biggest missteps: He paid premium pricing for office buildings located in a region already slumping due to the bursting of the tech bubble.

"Zell's success rate is not 100 percent," says Leupp, "but he's probably got one of the highest batting averages of all the great real estate investors."

BIG IS BETTER

Zell is also chairman of a third REIT, Manufactured Housing Communities, which owns or has an interest in more than 140 communities in 21 states.

"He loves the cash flow and demographic characteristics of manufactured home communities," Leupp notes. "They are essentially leased land, which is a very efficient way to own real estate. The asset class is not that big. It's highly fragmented, but rent and occupancy growth is very stable."

Of Zell's three companies, Manufactured Housing is the only one that does not dominate its asset class. With a market capitalization of $740.3 million, it trails Chateau Communities, which is why Zell made a second run at acquiring that company in 2003, having been rebuffed a few years earlier.

On the other hand, Equity Office, the country's largest REIT, with a market cap of $11 billion, is more than twice as big as its closest competitor in the same asset class. Equity Residential, the second largest REIT, with a market cap of $7.2 billion, holds a comfortable lead over the second largest multifamily REIT, Archstone-Smith Trust, which stands at $4.3 billion.

"Zell is a big proponent of the philosophy that size matters, especially in public companies," says Petrik. "With a bigger company you spread the overhead over a larger base and you drive down the costs of capital. After all, real estate is nothing more than a positive spread investing game."

Even before Zell took Equity Office public he was espousing the big-is-better philosophy. "The point is, if the competition stands at 6 million square feet and Equity Office is at 32 million square feet," Zell said just prior to the IPO, "we're going to go to 45 million square feet and they're going to go to 8 million square feet. Now let's talk about economies of scale. Let's talk about public company costs. Let's talk about financing costs. The idea that Equity Residential can go to the public market and do spot secondaries, and sell unsecured paper. All of these things are available to us because we're so big and we have such economy of scale."[21]

To which he added, "Let's assume that Equity Residential probably has a 50-basis-point advantage over anybody else. So now you put your apartment building up for sale. If I paid exactly the same as somebody else, I'd get a 9 percent return and he gets 8.5 percent. That's what's going on."[22]

Zell was convinced that bigger was better, and when he took his companies public, he just kept it up. "He realized that every time you increase in size, you open yourself up to a new set of investors," Petrik says. "I remember going into a meeting with a major fund manager who said, 'Here are my prerequisites, minimum investment of $100 million but no more than 5 percent of a company.' "

In the REIT world, that cuts the universe down to a handful of companies, including Equity Residential and Equity Office. "Zell realized the bigger you got, the better the liquidity in the shares and the more you opened yourself up to large institutional players," Petrik says.

THERE IS ALWAYS A WAY TO DO IT BETTER

Born in 1942 and raised in Chicago, Zell became interested in real estate at an early age. The story he likes to tell is about when he was at the University of Michigan and managed an Ann Arbor apartment complex for students. In exchange for rent, it was his job to fill the apartment building. He did this job so admirably, the owners gave him another complex to manage and started paying him as well. The management business, he used to say, was a good way to meet girls.

It was at the University of Michigan that he met his business partner, Bob Lurie, when they both pledged the same fraternity. In the mid-1960s, the two eventually assembled a mini-empire of apartment buildings in Ann Arbor.[23]

When asked, years later, if he was a long-term player, Zell responded, "I graduated from law school in 1966, I bought an apartment complex in Toledo, Ohio, in 1966. I paid off that mortgage in 25 years. I own it. There aren't many people who can say that."[24]

Always a bit ambitious, Zell concluded that Ann Arbor was not a big enough arena. "I was basically arrogant, and wanted to see what I could do in the real world," Zell said. "So, I sold the business to Lurie and said, 'When you get through screwing around and want to play with the big boys, call me.' " With that, Zell moved to Chicago. Lurie eventually saw the light and joined Zell in the Windy City two years later.

When Lurie arrived in Chicago, Zell had already put in motion his plan to syndicate real estate. After starting out as a minority partner, Lurie eventually became a full partner as the business grew.[25]

During the 1970s, Zell and Lurie bought ailing Midwest and Sunbelt properties, eventually selling for big gains. What Zell recognized then was that real estate was still an inefficient market and that he and Lurie could do it better.

"Zell is one of the greatest forces in the institutionalization of real estate. He is the godfather of modern institutional real estate," says Barden Gale, managing director of the real estate unit for ABP Investments U.S. The Netherlands-based ABP Investments ranks as one of the five largest pension funds in the world and is an active investor in U.S. real estate markets.

"People think there is nothing to operating real estate, you just own a bunch of bricks and people pay rent," Gale adds. "But Equity Residential and Equity Office are as good as it gets in modern real estate operating companies."

Although Zell might relish the appellation "grave dancer," what that actually means is that he is an extraordinary contrarian, gutsy investor, and one tough negotiator. Over time, he built up a balance sheet that provides him with staying power and, in many cases, pricing power in negotiations.

"He has been able to use leverage and that is why he negotiates an attractive price," says Leupp. "When he buys, he fixes the leasing problems, creates income from tenants, and then lets property values rise. Zell's companies only engage in a small amount of ground-up development. The majority of the value that his companies have created over the years has come from acquiring and improving existing buildings. In most cases his purchases have been well below replacement cost."

After the tech bubble burst and the low-interest-rate environment came to define the U.S. economy at the turn of the century, two things happened to seriously affect Zell's investments: Office demand quickly died, and vast amounts of square footage were thrown back on the market. In turn, office vacancies rose and rental rates dropped.

Also, the low-interest-rate environment allowed waves of apartment dwellers to become first-time homeowners, hurting the multi-family industry. Asked if he was worried about the economy, Zell responded with a resounding no, but added "I wouldn't say it's fun."[26]

As his REITs wallowed in weakening sectors, Zell stayed calm. "My focus," he says, "is the big picture: balance sheet, direction, and providing leadership to the senior teams. . . . We don't get paid to speculate. Stability is the objective."[27]

THE MAVERICK APPROACH TO BENEFITING FROM SOMEONE ELSE'S DISASTERS

1. Sometimes the best opportunities are found in the same spot you discovered them before.
2. Not all distressed property can be saved.
3. Know the land's true value and understand the concept of replacement cost.
4. The biggest opportunities come during the darkest times.
5. Figure out the competitive advantage you have over other new developments before buying.
6. The real diamonds in the rough usually look outwardly hopeless.
7. It is better to buy from a seller in financial distress than one with a deteriorating building. (For one thing, you won't have to invest as much additional money in rehabilitating the property.)
8. Figure out the seller's basic requirements and weaknesses early on in the negotiations.
9. Be a visionary and consider the property's future potential, which often isn't obvious on the surface.
10. Banks with distressed loans in foreclosure can be a good source of cheap property.
11. Sometimes it pays to partner up, especially if one of your partners is good at sniffing out great deals.
12. Have money ready so you can strike when an opportunity is pitched your way.

CHAPTER 8

Make Safe Gambles

Real estate investors are true gamblers. After all, there are no sure deals with any high-risk investment. But the Mavericks know how to mitigate the inherent risks. They do this by using a number of tactics, including conservative financing.

Real estate investing has always been a gamble. Speculators stalk property the way gamblers grab for a stack of cards. Developers are always rolling the dice. Like Las Vegas recidivists, real estate speculators—and often developers—never get to really enjoy the fruits of their labor because the winnings go into the next plot of land or apartment project.

Lenders often fuel this speculation by looking at past successes of the borrower and gladly handing out more money in the belief that their next project will be as good as the last. Sam Zell, chairman of both Equity Office Properties Trust and Equity Residential, theorizes that developers are like cocaine addicts, unable to stop building as long as lenders are there to dispense cash.[1] Perhaps *gambling addicts* would be the more appropriate metaphor to describe some real estate speculators.

For sure, successful property investors and developers do not avoid gambling, but they have learned to lessen the inherent risk as a way of improving their odds.

THINK AHEAD

What lenders have discovered, and what successful developers now know, is that you must forward-think a project. Instead of handing out cash based on the past successes of the developer, you must weigh the merits of each project based on how it might operate assuming development, market, and economic conditions go forward. Yes, it is true that the future cannot be ascertained, but there is enough data in the statistical tea leaves to guess which way things are headed.

Let us say, for example, that you wander across what looks to be a perfect location for a multifamily development and plunk down $1 million to buy it without doing due diligence on the market. With some research, you might learn that the biggest employer in the area is involved in a large financial scandal and that layoffs are in the future. Or you might find out that another big developer is building an apartment community less than a mile away. Perhaps job creation has reached a peak in the area and may soon crest. All of these factors could negatively affect your development and cannot be immediately recognized merely by looking at the past.

AVOID LOADING THE DATA

As any statistician will tell you, numbers can lie. People often use numbers to fit their own agendas. Neutrality is difficult when there is a strong intention—when you want a property very badly. Even those who should know better get caught in this tangle.

Zell, as chairman of Equity Office Properties Trust, was bearing down on another in a long line of his targets, Chicago-based Spieker Properties. Spieker is a large owner and operator of office buildings with a strong presence in such regions as California's Silicon Valley.

It was 2001. The technology bust was on and beginning to roil associated real estate markets around the country, especially those that were reliant on the technology business. Even with markets going in the wrong direction, Equity Office closed on Spieker, buying the company for a pricey $7.2 billion, including the assumption of $2.1 billion in debt and $431 million in preferred stock.[2]

Zell was betting on a short-lived adjustment to the faltering economy, especially on the West Coast. Even research houses climbed on board. In March 2001, Torto Wheaton Research chimed in, "Given how rents have spiked over the past five years in areas like San Francisco, San Jose, and New York, there would have to be a significant deterioration for this premium to disappear. We do not see this occurring."[3]

Unfortunately, it did. From the peak of the real estate cycle in the fall of 2000 to year-end 2002, office vacancy rates doubled nationally, while experiencing a negative net absorption for seven straight quarters. On the West Coast, San Francisco vacancy rates climbed to 21.9 percent, and San Jose's jumped to 19.8 percent (the U.S. average was 16.8 percent).[4]

Toward the end of 2002, Zell conceded he erred in buying Spieker at the top of the market and that rising vacancy rates caused what he called a "deterioration beyond our assumptions."[5]

Equity Office, the largest holder of office properties in the United States, has plenty of staying power to withstand the real estate downturn and even a few timing errors. Others do not. That's why so many developers and investors end up being financially castrated by cyclical downturns. Bankruptcy and forced sales are more common in the real estate business than are successes.

While true forward thinking based on good research helps reduce the risk in real estate, the best way to lessen the gamble is to rethink the financials.

Speculators will continue to speculate and developers will continue to develop through good times and bad. A prime piece of land in a top location coming on the market will attract those who can envision the next apartment development or industrial park. Visionaries will always be visionaries.

A SECURE CAPITAL STRUCTURE
IS YOUR BEST DEFENSE

The best way to reduce the gamble involved in real estate speculation is to control the backside of a deal—the dollar end. The template is conservative financing. Even a gambler like Donald Trump recommends understanding the downside to any deal and not doing it if you cannot afford the worst-case scenario.

To put it another way, John Kukral, president and chief executive officer of Blackstone Real Estate Advisors, the big New York–based opportunity fund, says, "When it comes down to it, the art of making money in real estate is having a capital structure that allows you to survive through downturns. For most of the people who lost money in real estate in the 1980s and early 1990s, if they could have held on, prices eventually came back."

To a developer or an experienced investor, the financials of any deal depend on a number of different factors: the amount of dollars brought to the transaction by the investor, the amount of money brought to the transaction by partners, and the amount offered by lenders.

The deal's sum total is determined by the value of the property in question, the amount of investor cash, the cost of borrowed money, the type of borrowed money, and the duration of borrowed money. Then there are the property factors such as projected cash flow and the cost of repairs, renovations, rebuilding, and reconstruction.

NO MONEY DOWN IS NOT A WINNING APPROACH

On the purchase end, conservative financing involves a reduction of leverage. This strategy obviously goes against the grain of traditional speculative deal making, which often involves as little equity involvement as possible. Indeed, real estate seminars hosted by so-called renowned speculators always tout no-money-down tactics.

This type of skinflint investing avoids the big picture and such issues as control and future development. Sam LeFrak, who died in April 2003 at the age of 85 following a long illness, built the Lefrak

MEET THE MAVERICKS

Samuel LeFrak

Birth Date: 1918 (died in 2003)

Occupation: Chairman, Lefrak Organization, New York, NY

Education: BS, business administration, University of
Maryland

Career Highlights:

- Constructs and develops Lefrak City in Queens, New York
- First developer to use New York bond-generated loans to build low-rent housing
- Builds thousands of low-cost cooperative and moderate rental housing throughout New York metro region
- Helps develop Battery Park City in lower Manhattan
- Honored by the United Nations for work with Habitat International
- Given "Distinguished Citizen of the World" award from United Nations

Organization into one of the world's largest private building companies of residential units. According to *Forbes* magazine's list of the "World's Billionaires," Sam LeFrak accumulated an estimated fortune of more than $2 billion. He always preferred to do business without relying on bank loans or government programs. He built his hallmark development—5,000 apartments known as Lefrak City in Queens, New York—using his own money to finance the project. "Like my other projects, Lefrak City was financed by the Lefrak

Organization. No government loans, tax rebates, nor special treatment," he liked to claim. "We bought the land, developed it, built on it, populated it, and continue to manage it."[6]

Still, for those so inclined, there are ways to lower leverage without digging deeper into your own pocket, including bringing in equity partners, mixing different types of loans, avoiding long-term landholds, and eschewing expensive debt.

Trammel Crow Residential (TCR), an Atlanta-based multifamily real estate firm, works hard to communicate the message to lenders and clients that its financial policy remains extremely conservative in regard to capital debt, open-ended construction loans, and land debt.

Despite having developed 150,000 apartment units across the country, TCR tries to avoid owning land for apartment development whenever possible. Its policy is to use TCR's own working capital to place land under contract and control it until long-term financing is in place.[7]

Similarly, TCR avoids using unsecured working capital lines to fund overhead or the costs of pursuing new projects. Consequently, it is extremely rare for the company to have outstanding working capital loans. When developing a new apartment complex, TCR requires its division partners to obtain permanent financing commitments or have significant equity in place before beginning construction of new projects. The idea is to avoid the risk of highly leveraged, open-ended constructions loans.[8]

This tactic is not much different than the business philosophy still used by the Lefrak Organization, which eschews construction loans on many of its projects, whether residential, office, or retail. Instead, the company obtains funding from a variety of equity sources, many of them internal. What is more, as a vertical company, Lefrak boasts its own general contracting operation that it uses for all of its projects. "Not only are we well organized, we have the capital to sustain ourselves," said Sam LeFrak. "We build our buildings without mortgages."[9]

FINANCE CONSERVATIVELY

If you finance conservatively enough, if the fundamentals are good, and if you can deliver value to a market in need of your particular type of product, over time your faith in a development will be justified, insists Richard LeFrak, who has served as president of the Lefrak Organization since 1975. (The only son of Sam LeFrak's four children, he is also the only one who entered the family business.) "But development can be treacherous business," Richard LeFrak admonishes. "Failures occur because developers don't have enough capital to sustain themselves if they misjudge a market. If things cost 20 or 30 percent over budget, the necessary financing to pay down loans and continue building is often impossible to find.

"My firm has managed to take some of the risk out of development by being conservative about financing and having the capital to sustain ourselves. During a soft period we are conservative about the use of cash. Sometimes we'll pay down debt even though it is conservative debt."

During good times, lenders accept easier credit, often allowing loan-to-value (LTV) ratios of 80 to 90 percent. (LTV is simply the ratio of the loan amount to the value of the property. Therefore, if the office building on the corner is selling for $1 million and the bank is willing to lend $800,000, it has an LTV ratio of 80 percent.) By taking a bigger gamble, the bank allows the borrower to increase his or her leverage. During down cycles, lenders tighten credit, and LTV ratios often fall below the 75 percent mark. Borrowers can make up the difference between what they can afford out of pocket and the bank loan with a mezzanine loan that bridges the difference between those two numbers. Such loans are called *mezzanines* because, in the event of a default, lenders inhabit the mezzanine position between the first mortgage and the equity (the buyer's contribution to the purchase amount). This is expensive money, with interest rates considerably higher than the first loan, but borrowers succumb to the lure, believing it is cheaper than raising more equity.

Obviously, with high loan-to-value deals, an investor's gamble becomes more risky, which is why with conservative financing—as Lefrak historically has achieved—investors move in the other direction. The Lefrak Organization tries to put 30 to 50 percent equity into a development, because it then has greater control over the property, also allowing for more flexibility. "If you are one of the developers that has the financial wherewithal to afford the massive equity commitment required when opportunities come up, you're not bidding against the whole world, just a few other smart and successful players," says Jamie LeFrak, Richard LeFrak's son and a managing director of the company.[10]

BIG GAMBLES CAN WORK IN BIG WAYS

The Lefrak Organization has been among the nation's major development gamblers when it comes to real estate, envisioning expansive projects of "cities within cities" on tracts of land that have been long ago discarded, abused, or considered too far out on the extreme of consciousness. Since five generations of LeFraks have been in the real estate business, it is difficult to pick the boldest builder in the family. But two individuals who come to mind are the ones who transformed the Lefrak Organization into the huge company it is today—the late Sam LeFrak and his son Richard.

If nothing else—and he accomplished a lot—Sam LeFrak became well known for the pioneering project, Lefrak City in the New York

City borough of Queens. This development brought much-needed middle-class housing to New York City in a massive way: twenty 18-story buildings with 5,000 apartments, sprawling across 40 acres of land.

Lefrak City is unique because it's almost a city unto itself. In addition to the apartments, the Lefrak Organization built 1 million square feet of commercial space, retail shops, leisure and entertainment facilities such as basketball, tennis, and soccer courts, swimming pools, libraries, houses of worship, and even vegetable gardens for residents to plant.[11]

By turning the first spade of ground for the project in 1960, Sam LeFrak took a tremendous gamble. But the man who was well known in the Big Apple for his ebullient personality was actually a fiscal conservative, a trait that served him well when putting together this landmark development.

The land that Sam LeFrak coveted was a swampy piece of ground running along the Long Island Expressway, cutting through the center of Queens. The property was owned by William Waldorf Astor, but that gave it no penumbra of esteem. In fact, it was once known as Mary's Dump, because people used to dump fill there. By the time LeFrak eyed the land, it still had abandoned Quonset huts on it where hundreds of World War II veterans and their families once lived.

"The negotiations with the trustees of the land were very protracted," explains Richard LeFrak, "because my father was willing to pay a certain amount of money and not a penny more."

Sam LeFrak's idea was to build this big complex without government assistance or tax abatements. "His goal was to build and be efficient about it," says Richard LeFrak.

His genius, wrote one Big Apple scribe, was in mass production—turning out apartment buildings the way Detroit turned out cars. Sam LeFrak figured he could keep costs down by not only buying a large tract of land where he could build en masse, but also by acquiring materials in huge quantities.[12]

Sam LeFrak took over the reigns of the Lefrak Organization in 1948. This was soon after World War II, when he could build one apartment building after another throughout New York City and its environs. He had a simple formula: If he could buy land at $1 a square foot near schools, the subway line, and shopping, he could make money while providing affordable shelter to keep middle-income families in the city.

This was still the post–World War II era. LeFrak understood that even 10 years after the war ended there was still a housing shortage for veterans. In response, he built specifically for the middle market—knowing there was always going to be a demand.

"It was like an assembly line in those days," says Richard LeFrak.

Sam LeFrak created economies of scale, and he passed this savings on to his tenants. "If apartments were renting for $100, he wanted to be able to rent profitably at $90," says Richard LeFrak. "He always said, 'I want to be fully rented right off. I will make it up because I build it more efficiently.' "

Although the Lefrak Organization has built everything from apartments to commercial high-rise towers, Sam LeFrak had an abiding affection for the multifamily product. "He was aggressive but quite conservative about our business," says Richard LeFrak. "What he didn't like about shopping centers and office buildings, for instance, was that right after you build them, everybody wants to lease space there. The next day, however, someone else builds a new office building or shopping center around the corner and yours is no longer so attractive. Building apartments in New York during the past 100 years was less of a challenge. There was always demand."

Because Sam LeFrak was not trying to attract economically upscale New Yorkers, Lefrak City—like several of his other developments— was aesthetically plain, built to human scale, and complete with a host of on-site amenities. LeFrak, who could voice a pithy epigram as fast as he could build apartments, once summed up the virtues of his apartments with this comment: "The windows opened and closed."[13] When the *New York Times*'s famed architectural critic Ada Louise Huxtable called LeFrak's buildings "ugly," he retorted, "She never built anything."[14]

When the community opened in 1961, it was New York's largest privately built housing project. To make sure all those millions of cars driving by on the Long Island Expressway knew what they were looking at, he erected a 120-foot billboard reading "Lefrak City." It is still known by that name today.

GAMBLE LIKE A MAVERICK

According to LeFrak history, the family's building roots began in France in the 1840s. It was Harry LeFrak who created a business in 1901 on this side of the Atlantic, building apartments for immigrants on Manhattan's Lower East Side.

In 1919, Harry LeFrak moved across the East River to build in Brooklyn, eventually shifting his focus to multifamily dwellings. Almost 30 years later, Harry appointed his son, Sam, as president of the firm. Sam began his task of launching the Lefrak Organization into the modern world, building thousands of low-cost, cooperative, and moderate-rental apartment houses throughout the New York metropolitan region, the rest of the United States, and even overseas.

"I produced an apartment every 16 minutes," Sam LeFrak liked to boast. "I took a page out of Detroit. I became the General Motors of building. I had my own forest and lumber mill, my own brick plant, my own gypsum, sand, and cement plants. I was 70 percent vertical and I could turn out my product at least a third cheaper than competitors."[15]

DON'T SELL JUST TO FINANCE THE NEXT PROJECT

Besides sheer volume, the biggest difference in the way Sam LeFrak ran the company, as opposed to his father, was his intent on holding what he built. Even today, many developers sell what they build for the cash to pay contractors for the next job. Sam LeFrak knew that if he could hold onto the assets he was creating, those assets would increase in value.

"I know from conversations I had with Father and with other people who worked with him in the old days that he would fight with my grandfather, Harry, about holding onto the properties," says Richard LeFrak. "Whatever Sam had to do he did in order to hold onto the buildings, because he knew they would be harder or impossible to replace."

He adds, "My family has a motto: If it's a good piece of real estate, it's not a crime to sell. It's a sin."

The LeFraks have always focused on the long term. Sam LeFrak's personal wealth was created over a long time period. "If you build into a mediocre market, sell right away, and plow the resulting profits into your next project immediately, you're selling yourself short," Sam LeFrak liked to say. The reason: Markets eventually turn, and long-term profits can be significantly greater than anything earned in the short term.

"Real estate is a long-term business," says Richard LeFrak. "Most of the developers who have been truly successful have been at it a long time, and they've been conservative about everything."

It does all add up. Holding onto real estate increases your net value, creates substantial collateral, and vastly improves your bargaining position with lenders, which should result in cheaper financing. Besides, if things turn really sour, a good diversified portfolio will go a long way toward keeping you afloat. Developers are often forced to sell off large portions of their portfolios to stave off lenders clamoring to be repaid when real estate recessions hit, as they often do in this cyclical industry.

Sam LeFrak's way was to build and hold.

By 1991, it was said that one in every 16 New Yorkers had at some point lived in a Lefrak unit. The company was ranked as one of the largest private real estate companies in the world. Starting with Sam's father, the Lefrak Organization has built thousands of apartments plus millions of square feet of commercial and retail space. Today, the Lefrak Organization is made up of 60 percent residential and 40 percent commercial developments. The company's total square footage rests at 40 million square feet, with a very high percentage in the New York metropolitan area.

Like his father before him, Richard LeFrak came into the business while still a student in high school. He was elevated to the position of president in 1975. But Richard had been walking the rounds at projects with his dad since he was 13 years old.

Born in 1945 and raised in New York, Richard LeFrak graduated cum laude from Amherst College in 1967 and studied law at Columbia University, from which he received his doctor of law degree in 1970. Soon after, he was given responsibility for a new development. "One of my first ventures was in Somerset, New Jersey, where there was a community of single-family homes. A local developer controlled several acres and had managed to zone it for a high-rise apartment building. The guy couldn't get the thing financed," Richard LeFrak recalls. "It was an attractive New Jersey neighborhood. I could see the potential because nearby was Rutgers University, a major hospital facility, and an expanding area for a pharmaceutical-based industrial complex. So we negotiated to obtain the property, developed a high-rise apartment building, and we still have it today. It has always been a very successful part of our residential portfolio."

Most developers, if they work hard enough and are lucky, do just one self-contained landmark project over a lifetime. The

MEET THE MAVERICKS

Richard LeFrak

Birth Date: 1945
Occupation: President, LeFrak Organization, New York, NY
Education: BS, economics, Amherst College; JD, Columbia University

Career Highlights:
- Initiates New York City's Westside Urban Renewal Program
- Supervises construction and completion of the Gateway Plaza phase of Battery Park City
- Continues to develop the 600-acre Newport project across the Hudson River from Manhattan, including more than 4,000 residential units
- In conjunction with Simon Property Group, develops 2 million square feet of retail in Newport
- Newport success spurs Wall Street companies to move back-office operations to Jersey City

Lefrak Organization has done several. Soon after Lefrak City was completed—early in Richard LeFrak's tenure as president of the company—the firm's second major community was undertaken.

As the World Trade Towers were being constructed on lower Manhattan's West Side during the early 1970s, the Port Authority of New York and New Jersey, which was building the Towers, decided the huge amount of dirt being excavated would be used to create a 92-acre landfill in the Hudson River on which Battery Park City was to be built.

The Port Authority wanted to build apartments on the landfill that would entice residents to an area made up almost entirely of office towers. "The concept was to have a self-sustaining community," says Richard LeFrak. The Lefrak Organization was invited to participate as a codeveloper.

Occasionally, companies stumble into bad situations, not because the property is not right or the general market conditions are not good, but because regulators have crimped original plans. "The project was eventually very successful but with the city and State of New York's heavy involvement," says Richard LeFrak, "it was a political football from the start.

"We started on the project when there was nothing, and there were stops and starts until the late 1970s. Then there was a question of liens and liabilities. To prove there was life in the project, we went ahead and built the first apartments—1,700 units called Gateway Plaza—along with retail stores, the Hudson River Esplanade, an underground parking garage, and a health and swim club. Having got the project started, there was a good chance that New York state, which was having major fiscal problems, would put the whole thing into bankruptcy. The state owned the ground and leased it to us."

Sam LeFrak enjoyed telling this tale: "I was building affordable housing, as part of phase one, when along comes Governor Hugh Carey of New York and he wants to put the job into receivership. So I went to Carey and said, 'Hey, wait a minute. I've been here 18 years. I filled the land. I built here. What do you mean you want to put it into bankruptcy? [You've] got $200 million of people's money here.' Carey agreed, and I went ahead and built phase one."[16]

Then there was the problem of vision. Politicians were becoming insecure about the project because that part of Manhattan has been recognized as a commercial-financial district with little or no street life after working hours. The Lefrak Organization rightly assumed the project would be quite successful because the majority of people the company surveyed and its own market studies indicated the community would be rented by middle-class professionals who would be able to walk to work as well as commute conveniently to other parts of the city. Moreover, from the LeFrak's own building experience it was anticipated that Battery Park City would evolve into its own self-sustaining community.

Battery Park City was supposed to be for middle-income renters and buyers, but state housing authorities determined along the way to create a more luxurious neighborhood.[17]

The company, which always built for the middle class, fought with the housing authority over the direction of the Battery Park City. Finally, in the early 1980s, the Lefrak Organization quit the project altogether. Afterward, Sam LeFrak said to the press, "I told them, 'I don't believe in taking care of the rich and famous. I believe in serving the people.' "[18]

Later, he explained it in simpler terms: "They started dealing from the bottom of the deck. We said, '*arrivederci*.' "[19]

Battery Park City eventually opened to the public in 1983, just about the time the Lefrak Organization was about to enter one of the largest gambles ever undertaken by a U.S. developer.

In 1983, two shopping center developers, Melvin Simon and Herb Glimcher, were looking to build a shopping mall in Jersey City, an industrial city in New Jersey just across the Hudson River from lower Manhattan. The builder they called upon was the Lefrak Organization. "My father went out there," Richard LeFrak fondly remembers. "He was 65 years old and he phoned me at once from the site and said, 'Richard, I have been dreaming about something like this my whole life. You have to see it.' So I went out there to see for myself. I saw nothing but industrial buildings, warehouses, abandoned piers, and rusting railroad tracks—no streets, no neighborhood, no infrastructure."

Richard, however, also observed what his father saw. They were standing one mile from the water facing Manhattan. Nearby was a

PATH subway station that connected the area to both lower and midtown Manhattan with tracks running under the Hudson River. "We were five minutes from the World Trade Towers and Wall Street, 10 minutes from Penn Station," says Richard LeFrak.

The LeFraks envisioned something vast, something vital. Newport, as it is called, eventually was and is just that: a 600-acre master-planned, mixed-use community, consisting of retail, residential, office, leisure, and entertainment facilities, all located along Jersey City's Hudson River waterfront, opposite the Wall Street area of Manhattan.

Just acquiring the land meant dealing with 157 different land-owners.

"Jersey City was a blue-collar town where the politics were volatile," recalls Richard LeFrak. "Along the river were vast tracts of land owned by the railroads. The port business had abandoned the old railroad terminals and deteriorating piers to move south to Elizabeth and Port Newark. It was so depressing. The land could be bought at the right price because at the time it was not worth too much."

Other developers looked at the potential of the area, but it was obvious that to build there would mean creating a new neighborhood where none had existed. It was an awesome and tremendous challenge.

Construction began in 1986. By 2003, about the half of the estimated $10 billion project had been developed. That included some 4,000 apartments, a shopping mall, shopping centers, schools, 5 million square feet of office space, a hotel, marina, restaurants, ferry landing, and the Hudson Waterfront Walkway. The Lefrak Organization also laid in some of the infrastructure, including sewers, power, and roads, as well as upgrading the old PATH subway station.

According to the *Newark Sunday Star-Ledger,* the average household income in Newport is $109,351 compared to $45,245 for the rest of Jersey City and $47,220 for all of Hudson County. Residents are more likely to be single, renters, and foreign-born (43.1 percent are Asian). In addition, 83 percent of Newport residents are college grads, compared to 28 percent for Jersey City and 30 percent for the state of New Jersey.

LARGE DEVELOPMENTS CREATE VALUE IN UNDEVELOPED LAND

As Richard LeFrak reflects, "This was a very high risk project. Even after 17 years, we are not done yet. The thing to remember as you develop the land is that the real estate you haven't touched has now gone up in value because you have built a community."

As the Lefrak Organization developed acres of vacant land, the remaining acreage grew in value. Since the company didn't change the capital structure of the project from the beginning, as it continued to build and values were being established, the company became increasingly more—not less—conservative.

The difference between a real estate investor and a builder, according to Richard LeFrak, is that investors gamble on the market and the financing. When they buy an asset, at least they know what it will cost. Conversely, if you are a builder, you don't know what the development will eventually cost. That is the big risk. However, you can increase your odds by building efficiently. "On big sites, we build on a large scale, taking advantage of the efficiencies," he says.

USE CONSERVATIVE FINANCING TO REDUCE RISK

The Lefrak Organization was able to reduce its risk from the start by taking a conservative approach to financing. "With a project this size, we knew it would take a long time and we couldn't just depend on a hot market to bail us out. We had been very conservative in how we financed the buildings. We always utilized what I consider to be lower leverage compared to how other developers operate. We're not sellers. We think of business in a generational way. I don't burden myself with the baggage of worrying about how much I can make on a property since I don't have a stock price to consider."

In the development business, Richard LeFrak observes, the high end of risk is in the building. At first it is difficult to estimate exactly what a project will cost. You might estimate $50 million, but it could actually come in at $40 million or even $60 million or more. To balance that inherent risk, you have to be conservative in the initial appraisal of the development's potential. And you need a good capital structure.

"Bottom line," says Richard LeFrak, "is when a building is finished and ready to be rented, the best that we can do is deliver good value to our customers."

If there's one thing Richard LeFrak is sure of, it is that the apartment business in the New York metropolitan area is always steady, if not rock solid. Indeed, at Newport, the company's first nine high-rise apartment buildings (over 4,000 units) and a new 443-unit condominium building were quickly 100 percent occupied.

While the office market is always subject to market conditions and the vicissitudes of the economy, Lefrak's first five mid- and high-rise office buildings at Newport have also done very well, attracting such tenants as UBS/Paine Webber, CIGNA, U.S. Trust, and J.P. Morgan Chase, Morgan Stanley, and Charles Schwab.

There are a number of ways to mark the success of Newport, but on a financial basis, half of the land that is still undeveloped is not burdened by any third-party debt. "This is a luxury for us," says Richard LeFrak. "We can now sit back and ask ourselves, 'Is this the right time to start the next development, or should we wait?' " When you have no immediate financing obligations, time is on your side.

THE MAVERICK APPROACH TO MAKING SAFE GAMBLES

1. Know that real estate investing is a risky proposition.
2. Take steps to minimize the downside and improve your odds.
3. Forward-think your project. In other words, consider what the area and property might look like in the future, not just now.
4. Avoid prejudicing the research. Remain neutral, even when your heart is set on a particular piece of real estate.
5. Use a secure capital structure as your best defense against future unforeseen difficulties.
6. Be conservative when it comes to financing.
7. No money down is not the best strategy.
8. Big gambles can result in big payoffs.
9. Look for the potential in unloved property that no one else can sell. Just don't overpay for it.
10. Create economies of scale and pass the savings on to your tenants. You'll make more money and this will give you a competitive advantage.
11. Do not sell immediately just to finance the next deal.
12. A large-scale project creates its own value.

CHAPTER 9

Hire Savvy Managers

Acquiring real estate is only the beginning. Once the papers have been signed and you own the property, you must figure out the best way to manage it. Bad management can quickly doom an otherwise good investment. If you decide to become a property or asset manager, take these tasks very seriously.

In early 2003, Steven Lowy addressed a group of Sydney pension investors. Lowy is a managing director of Westfield Holdings Limited, an international real estate company based in Australia. During his lengthy speech, he highlighted a number of factors for his company's longtime success, not the least of which was property management.

"We recognize that raising the capital is only part of the story," Lowy noted. "We believe that the ability to manage the underlying real estate is just as important, regardless of how you are structured."[1]

For a company such as Westfield Holdings, which derives its main income from the Australian-listed real estate investment trusts Westfield America Trust and Westfield Trust, property management is everything. The companies collectively own 113 shopping centers and malls in Australia, Europe, and the United States. The cumulative value of those centers stands at more than $18 billion. Westfield has clearly found a way to effectively manage its far-flung empire.

There are two ways to manage your investment properties: Hire a third party, or do it yourself.

People and institutions that are just *investors*—those with no desire to develop, lease, or arrange for janitorial services—hire third-party managers. There is nothing wrong with that. Big institutional investors, whether pension funds or investment banks, go into property investments knowing full well they have no intention of actively managing the real estate. That is why companies such as CB Richard Ellis, Grubb & Ellis, Jones Lang LaSalle, and many others were created. They are professional managers with the experience, insight, and contacts to do an excellent job.

On the other hand, *entrepreneurs*—those either just beginning to create a portfolio of properties or those who are actively developing—

often prefer to do the property management themselves. This decision could be based on economics (it is cheaper not to have to hire an outside party) or knowledge (you feel comfortable that you have the skills to do this job).

DUAL MANAGEMENT CAN WORK

While investors with a few properties (or even one) view management as a total immersion of on-site tasks, such as making sure the air-conditioning is functioning or a leaky roof is repaired, large holders of real estate divide the two tasks. On-site chores, including leasing, are generally lumped under the formal category of *property management*. Investing, positioning, and selling the property come under the less definitive term of *asset management*. In many instances, the property manager and asset manager are two totally different companies.

A fully vertical real estate company such as Westfield (the sum of all its parts) takes the approach that in real estate, it is better to integrate these two functions. "From finance to development to management, a company needs to be integrated because one shouldn't put a part of operations totally outside the system," says Peter Lowy, a managing director of Westfield Holdings. "An asset manager should not be looking at a property without understanding what the management issues are and what the market issues are. If you separate these functions, property management and asset management go down different paths."

This is reinforcing for the small investor, who generally has to do it all, but probably wishes he or she could afford to hire someone else to manage the property. If the portfolio does grow, it might be worthwhile to develop those skills in-house.

Steven Lowy, Peter's brother, somewhat more elegantly explains the virtues of integration this way: "The long-term viability of the investment depends on us [Westfield] taking 'ownership' of that investment in a very real sense, and managing it in a holistic way— at a strategic level, but also right down to the micro, day-to-day decisions affecting the income streams of the real estate—in our case, shopping centers."[2]

Bedford Property Investors, a Lafayette, California, industrial and office REIT, works in a similar manner as Westfield. It believes the long-term value of its properties is enhanced through in-house management. It directly manages almost all of its real estate, conducting asset and property management through regional offices.[3]

ATTEND TO THE NEEDS OF TENANTS FIRST

Whether outsourcing management to a professional real estate management company or doing those chores within the company, the same principles apply. In regard to properties already in the portfolio, the costs (tenant improvements, leasing commissions, loss of income due to vacancy) associated with tenant turnover can eventually prove to be very expensive, so it is often best to address the needs of existing tenants first.

Good property management starts with retention. That obviously means being quick to respond to tenant needs, solving occasional problems, and addressing a new lease very early in the process. Less obvious, but also essential, is the need to ascertain accurate data on all properties in the market area. It's important to know what the competition may offer a client when a lease is coming to an end. Attending to existing tenant needs can increase retention, thereby making properties more attractive to new tenants.

STANDARDIZE PROCEDURES AND ESTABLISH A REPORTING SYSTEM

Again, even for a small investor, it is important to create a formalized approach to management, including standardized procedures, documents, and reports. This is especially true as your portfolio grows. Information concerning a group of properties has to be understandable and comparative.

Properly developed templates for key forms such as term sheets and purchase and lease agreements can greatly accelerate transactions and cut costs. Similarly, documenting procedures and goals increases the likelihood that transactions in different parts of a city, state, or in other parts of the country will be processed in a timely fashion.

Some items to consider: monthly operating reports and, if there are outside investors, quarterly reports that include information gleaned from the operating reports. Standardization of processes could also include procedures for ordering title work, surveys, environmental reports, accounting documentation, and bank forms.

The long-term value of properties is enhanced by attention to detail and hands-on service. That includes leasing activities, maintenance and repairs, cleaning, coordination of outside service providers, financial record keeping, rent collection, and operating expense payouts.[4]

When there are varied properties in numerous locations, the question becomes, how do you get control of it all? Peter Lowy has a simple answer: systemization. "It depends on the operating system, which includes the information system, leasing system, billing system, and so on," he says. "We obviously have everything structured."

STAY ATTUNED TO LOCAL ISSUES

"The key is, how do you run a global company that, in essence, has local issues? If you are in Australia, how do you know what the issues are in Seattle?" Peter Lowy asks. The same could be asked of a local entrepreneur. If you are on the west side of the city, how do you know what the issues are on the east side?

The answer to all these questions is the same, according to Peter Lowy. "Management has to be very focused on the local issue on the ground at the local center." In addition, local residents need the authority to act responsibly. With Westfield, managers at local malls, development directors, and so forth are given wide latitude in problem solving and are encouraged to make important decisions.

"You need to give everybody in the chain of command the authority to make decisions," says Peter Lowy. "We have guidelines as to how these decisions can fit within our corporate atmosphere. Nevertheless, the manager in Seattle or Los Angeles must have the authority to deal with local issues and needs us to back them on the decisions they make. They deal with the local issues within the guidelines corporate management sets."

BE FLEXIBLE AND ADAPT TO EXTERNAL MARKET CHANGES

Systems and procedures create an overarching management approach, but in the world of real estate, outside events continually infringe on planning. Therefore, it is important not to be too rigid. Even a company as big and widespread as Westfield tries to be adaptive to the myriad circumstances that arise daily.

"Our management psyche is to look at each market through

global eyes and then adapt it for local conditions," says Steven Lowy. "This means we are prepared to try new things and keep our minds open about what's possible in a given market, not just blindly work the local conditions in terms of our structure or management style."[5]

The greatest long-term cost savings arise from a company's ability to learn the lessons of the past and apply those lessons to making future transactions more efficient and cost effective. That is why a management program must continually reevaluate to find new ways to manage costs and improve the process.[6]

ADOPT A TIME MANAGEMENT PROGRAM

Property management involves so many individual tasks that it can literally steal away too much of your time even if your portfolio consists of a single, multitenant building such as a small apartment duplex or strip center. The individual jobs should include rent collection, repairs, contract renewal, maintenance, supplier and vendor transactions, bookkeeping, contracting external services from municipalities, financial reporting, emergency needs, tenant evictions, and occasional site visits.

The best way to deal with all this is to create a daily, weekly, and monthly schedule with enough flexibility to handle the occasional emergency. It also helps to prioritize these tasks in terms of importance and allot a budget. Inconsistent management can bleed an investment of profitability.

Once scheduling and a budget are established for one property, if an investor remains active in the same asset class, subsequent investments should be easier. As services, supplies, and time allocations are spread over numerous investments, the cost of management per square foot declines.

ALWAYS HAVE AN EXIT STRATEGY

Although your objective may be to maintain ownership of the investment for a long time, at some point in the future the property may have to be sold. Active day-to-day management should always reflect the value potential of the property if and when it is put on the market. The general idea is to maintain the property with maximum effort to retain rental income and occupancy rates.

Some key points to keep in mind: Establish good tenant relations through responsive management; develop appropriate marketing and pricing strategies; operate and maintain a comfortable working environment for building occupants through a regular monthly maintenance program; implement a risk management plan; budget for capital improvements to increase functionality and marketability; and be prepared to do a complete financial analysis.[7]

THE BEST INVESTMENT MAY BE REDEVELOPING AN EXISTING PROPERTY

After a lengthy and often bitter hostile takeover battle, Rodamco North America, a Netherlands-based property company with a portfolio of malls in the United States, was forced to give up its independence. In January 2002, Westfield America, Simon Property Group, and the Rouse Company signed a definitive agreement to jointly purchase the assets of Rodamco for $5.3 billion. For leading the assault on Rodamco, Westfield came out of the deal with 14 shopping centers in five states at a cost of $2.3 billion.

Westfield America was busy in 2002. That year it also bought nine regional shopping centers from Cleveland-based Richard E. Jacobs Group for about $750 million. After owning just seven U.S.

malls in 1993, when the shopping spree was over, the company found itself with 61 retail centers in its shopping bag. (Since those two big transactions, Westfield America acquired two more centers.) It had clearly become a major player in the U.S. shopping mall industry.

Westfield's theory is buy, redevelop, and hold. It then looks at the property again and redevelops it once more. One of the first shopping malls the company acquired in the United States was located in Connecticut. That mall is still under Westfield ownership and has been redeveloped five times since its acquisition in 1977. As another example, in 1986 Westfield purchased a mall in Paramus, New Jersey. "It was the third of five regional malls in the market when we bought it," says Peter Lowy, "and we expanded it twice. Now it is 2 million square feet." In 2003, Westfield began planning a third redevelopment on the center.

In the Rodamco deal, Westfield saw from the start that redevelopment costs would eventually total about $1.5 billion. "Redevelopment was one of the major issues in that portfolio," says Peter Lowy. "It was the reason we went after it. We believed the real estate and assets were nowhere near maximum potential."

One of the key properties in the Rodamco deal was the San Francisco Shopping Center in San Francisco. "We said there was real potential for redevelopment there," says Peter Lowy. Rodamco, fighting off a hostile move against its portfolio, claimed there was no room for redevelopment because it was boxed in. But within six months of buying the portfolio, Westfield America entered into a joint development venture with Forest City Enterprises, the Cleveland-based mall company, which owned the building next door. The joint venture will create an additional 350,000 square feet of specialty shops, 235,000 square feet of office space, a 3,200-seat theater, and a 340,000-square-foot Bloomingdales.

"We saw the potential," Peter Lowy says. "We knew it was not at full value. And that is the essence of our business—creating value by development of the portfolio or centers we purchase. The same held true for the Jacobs acquisition. One of the reasons we bought it was because of the redevelopment potential. The nine centers we bought were the higher echelon in the portfolio, but they still needed a bunch of work."

Until the real estate recession of the late 1990s, American developers built and then built anew. It was rare that a shopping center or mall developer went back to original projects. In Australia, however, the major cities are highly urbanized and there is not a great deal of room in populated areas. The key there was to always redevelop and expand existing centers. When Westfield began buying in the United States, it continued to do so.

"It was incredible to come from Australia and see a mall built on 75 acres of land," says Peter Lowy. "There is so much land with these centers, with their immense parking fields, you rarely ever have to buy additional land."

Westfield looks to invest about 50 percent of the capital the company spent buying the portfolio into redeveloping it. According to Peter Lowy, "We create our own development pipeline." He cautions that this is not a matter of buying things cheap. "Even if you pay the full, or right, price for an asset, you can still reinvest capital and make it a better asset, and after the redevelopment, you can increase your return."

Here is another way to look at redevelopment as it fits into a company's general strategy: When Frank Lowy, chairman and founder of the Westfield companies, addressed a general meeting of Westfield Holdings Limited members in 2002, he said, "Growth in assets under management, either through acquisition or redevelopment, leads directly to increased profitability for Westfield Holdings through an immediate increase in property and funds management income, and in the medium to longer term, an increase in development income."[8]

Toward the end of 2002, after the Rodamco and Jacobs portfolios were integrated, Frank Lowy noted, "We put in place Westfield systems and branding and stamped our management style on the properties. The occupancy levels in these new U.S. centers increased by almost a percentage point—to 90.4 percent—since we took over the management of the centers just six months ago. Again, this reflects our intensive approach to leasing and ongoing demand from retailers for the quality space we provide."[9]

START SMALL

The story of Frank Lowy, founder of the Westfield group of companies, is one of the more fascinating in the annals of modern real estate aggregation.

Born in Slovakia in 1930, his family moved to Hungary when World War II broke out. He and most of his family survived the Holocaust. When the war was finally over, he attempted to emigrate to Palestine only to find himself interned by the British in Cyprus. After finally making it to Palestine, he joined the Haganah and fought in Israel's war for independence.

Frank Lowy's mother, eldest brother, and sister had emigrated to Australia. In 1952, after not seeing his family for six years, he went to visit them in Sydney. He decided to stay despite the fact that he barely spoke any English and was, in fact, penniless, having borrowed money to make the long journey.

His first job was driving a truck delivering deli foods. During this time, he met John Saunders, an immigrant from Hungary, and the two decided to open their own deli in the outer Sydney suburb of Blacktown. It was one of those perfect matches. Frank Lowy and John Saunders remained partners in a number of ventures for three decades.

MEET THE MAVERICKS

Frank Lowy

Birth Date: 1930

Occupation: Chairman of Westfield Holdings, Ltd., Westfield America Trust, and Westfield Trust, Sydney, Australia

Education: No degree

Career Highlights:

- Joins Haganah and fights in Israel's war for independence
- Exports U.S. shopping center experience to Australia
- Takes Westfield Development Corporation public; becomes known as Westfield Holdings Ltd.
- Buys shopping center in Connecticut, then expands globally
- Creates two publicly traded real estate investment trusts: Westfield America Trust and Westfield Trust

In the years after World War II, Sydney's metro population grew exponentially, fueled by massive immigration from all parts of Europe. While the deli proved successful, Lowy and Saunders took notice when a developer bought land nearby and built several shops. That seemed like a better idea than the deli, so they sold out, bought some land, and subdivided it. Some of the acreage was sold to home builders; the rest was used for a small hotel and retail. In 1959, their first shopping center opened.

A year later, Frank Lowy took a trip to California. While traveling around, he noticed all the new development going on in the state, especially on the retail side. Upon returning, he decided retail development should be the company's future. In a very real sense, Lowy exported the U.S. shopping center experience to Australia—with a couple of cultural differences.

In 1960, Westfield Development Corporation listed on the Sydney Stock Exchange. The capitalization from the public offering helped Westfield get a running start during the 1960s, which, as in the United States, was a boom period for developers.

The difference in retail development between the two countries was significant in terms of tenants, however. The rise of shopping malls in the United States revolved around key anchors—big department stores. Australia development followed the English model, where the department stores stayed in downtowns. As a result, key anchors in Australia were the fast-growing supermarket chains.

Westfield began building a number of supermarkets, selling the buildings to the chains. It soon realized that better returns could be achieved if it bought the land, built the supermarket, and then leased the store and land to the chain, while at the same time adding mall shops. "That is how the mall business developed in Australia," Peter Lowy explains. "It was on the back of the supermarkets. Even the enclosed malls today in Australia have a full line of supermarkets and discount stores."

As Westfield grew, there was only so much it could do in Australia, which despite its large land mass boasts a population of only 19 million. In 1977, Westfield bought its first shopping center in the United States—in Trumbull, Connecticut.

FIND AN APPROPRIATE CORPORATE STRUCTURE

Entrepreneurial real estate investors, especially those who have found a way to hold on to early developments, eventually grow their businesses into larger, more complex companies. The trick, then, is to find a corporate structure that allows for management and expansion.

Some very large companies remain private and family owned, but other successful entrepreneurs try to find a structure that fairly values the holdings of the company. This was the quandary Westfield faced at the end of the 1970s. As it began to invest internationally, it would face this quandary again.

In 1979, Westfield Development consisted of one publicly traded company. It owned all the malls and did all its own development and management. Unfortunately, the end of the 1970s in Australia was a time of high interest rates, and it was impossible to borrow money if a company was highly leveraged, which Westfield was.

"There were two things going on; the company couldn't raise capital to grow, and it was very undervalued," says Peter Lowy, "So, what we did was separate the company into two parts, Westfield Holdings, which would do the management and development, and Westfield Property Trust, a property trust [the Australian version of a real estate investment trust] that would hold the owned real estate."

The day before the transaction, Westfield held a capitalization of A$74 million, recalls Peter Lowy. "The day after the transactions, the combined capitalization of the two companies was A$205 million. The difference was, the value of the real estate was not being recognized in the old company, but came through when listed as a separate stock."

A decade later, Westfield tried to find an appropriate, separate structure for its then-growing American portfolio. Its first attempt was Westfield International, which owned the U.S. assets, but that was quickly delisted and privatized. Finally, Westfield America Trust was created in 1996 and taken public in Australia.

Today, the Westfield group consists of three separately listed companies: Westfield Holdings Limited (the group's management and funds management provider, which delivers design, development, construction, leasing, marketing, and management services to the shopping centers and is also the funds manager for the property trusts); Westfield Trust (Australia's largest publicly traded property trust with interests in 42 shopping centers in Australia and New Zealand); and Westfield America Trust (Australia's second-largest property trust, which invests in U.S. real estate). In 2000, Westfield expanded into the United Kingdom. This growing portfolio is owned by Westfield Holdings.

"Our business philosophy is for Westfield Holdings to make the initial investments in a market and, when it reaches a critical mass, raise equity capital to expand the business in that market," Peter Lowy says. "We are planning a financial exercise where Westfield Holdings will sell down its position in the United Kingdom to other U.K. investors or float a third REIT in Australia purely for U.K. development."

Management is still a family business. Frank Lowy has three sons, the oldest of whom, David, runs a private investment company called the Lowy Family Group. He also sits as a vice-chairman of the Westfield Holdings board. The two younger sons, Peter and Steven, are integrally involved with the companies.

Peter, born in 1959, holds a bachelor of commerce degree from the University of New South Wales. After working in the investment banking field in the United States and United Kingdom, he joined Westfield in 1983 and today serves as managing director of Westfield Holdings and Westfield America Trust. He lives in Los Angeles.

Steven, born in 1962, followed his brother to the University of New South Wales, also earning a bachelor of commerce degree, with honors, and then moved into the U.S. investment banking industry. In 1997, he became a managing director of Westfield Holdings and Westfield America Trust and is based in Australia.

Fortunately, the two brothers work well together, which is as it

MEET THE MAVERICKS

Peter and Steven Lowy

Birth Dates: Peter, 1959
Steven, 1962

Occupation: Peter: Managing Director of Westfield Holdings
Ltd., Westfield America Trust, and Westfield Trust,
Los Angeles, CA
Steven: Managing Director of Westfield Holdings
Ltd., Westfield America Trust, and Westfield Trust,
Sydney, Australia

Education: Peter: Bachelor of Commerce, University of New
South Wales
Steven: Bachelor of Commerce, University of New
South Wales

Career Highlights:

- List Westfield America Trust in Australia
- Oversee selection of Westfield America to manage retail component of World Trade Center in New York
- Buy nine regional shopping centers from Richard E. Jacobs Group
- Lead takeover battle for Rodamco North America; acquiring 14 shopping centers
- Join the fight to take over Taubman Centers
- Launch A$1.9 billion takeover bid for the AMP Shopping Centre Trust, owner of nine Australian malls

should be considering they are comanaging directors of the same property trust.

"We used to split the business on geographical grounds, but that proved difficult. Now we split it on operating grounds," Peter Lowy says. "Steven, in Australia, has all the operating side of the business, the management and development worldwide, and I, in Los Angeles, have all the finance and corporate activity worldwide."

The idea is to better integrate different facets of the business. "If he sees things in Australia or England or the United States, then we can adopt it in Australia, England, or the United States," Peter Lowy explains. "If there is a situation in Seattle, he can see it in a different way than it has been dealt with in the United States. We can take an international perspective to local issues and deploy that perspective in dealing with them locally."

INTEGRATE ALL PARTS OF THE ORGANIZATION

To operate an expanding real estate enterprise, whether locally, regionally or even globally, the key is to keep all parts of the operation in mesh. As Peter Lowy says, "We believe you need to integrate."

He explains: "From finance to development to management, the company needs to be integrated because you cannot have some part of it totally outside the system. We do something most of our competitors don't do: We integrate the day-to-day operations and development, which means we have our own in-house architecture, our own design work, and our own general contractors."

That is done through a team. Westfield uses a global executive committee, headed by Frank Lowy in Australia.

Integration also means combining the on-the-ground issues with organizational procedures. While Westfield uses the same operating and management systems worldwide, Peter Lowy contends the key to running an expanding company is still to follow all of the local issues, where the property is located. "We take the local issues and integrate them into the global company," he explains.

DO THINGS DIFFERENTLY

As a large operator of shopping malls, Westfield does a number of things differently than, for example, most large shopping mall operators in the United States.

First, it brands its malls. Whether in Sydney, Melbourne, Los Angeles, or St. Louis, a Westfield mall is identifiable by the brand "Westfield Shoppingtown."

Second, the company prefers to invest in markets rather than in malls. That means the company likes to have a group of regional malls in large metroplexes—Westfield boasts 12 malls in Los Angeles; six malls in San Diego, St. Louis and Ohio; four in Florida and Connecticut; and three in suburban Washington, D.C., and Maryland.

Third, because it is a global company, it tries to keep its eyes open for what Steven Lowy calls "formats that have not traditionally been on the radar screen of the U.S. mall industry." This can pertain to operations as well. Steven Lowy uses occupancy as an example. "Traditional occupancy levels in U.S. malls have been in the high 80s/low 90s. The U.S. market has lived with these levels for years. In Australia, we have traditionally achieved 99 percent occupancy."[10]

ADOPT SUCCESSFUL STRATEGIES EMPLOYED ELSEWHERE

There is a surprisingly great deal of market differentiation between the United States and Australia. Still, Westfield found it hard to contend with the anomaly in occupation levels. As a result, it has focused very hard on getting numbers higher in the United States. Today its American investment portfolio boasts an occupancy rate of around 94 percent.

There is another difference between Australia and the United States. In the latter country, department stores have been the anchor of choice ever since the indoor shopping mall was invented. In Australia, malls are anchored by a combination of discount stores, department stores, and supermarkets, so Westfield had been adding to its mix in the United States with discounters such as Wal-Mart and Target—and even with destination stores such as Galyans.

"We keep our minds open about other formats," Steven Lowy says. Recent redevelopments by Westfield did not revolve solely around department stores, but have focused more on the introduction and improvement of entertainment, food, and lifestyle retailers that are expected to give greater depth to the customer experience.[11]

STAY THE COURSE, EVEN IN TOUGH TIMES

At the start of 2003, Westfield America may only have ranked as the fourth-largest shopping center owner in the United States, based on gross leasable space, but it was the second-largest shopping center owner in the world. In 2003, its ultimately unsuccessful joint takeover bid with Simon Property Group for Taubman Centers was moving steadily through the court system—and it was a very contentious hostile takeover effort. The Taubman portfolio consists of 21 superregional malls in nine states.

At the time of this writing, Westfield Trust had also launched an A$1.9 billion takeover bid for the AMP Shopping Centre Trust, which if successful, will give Westfield interests in another six malls. This will bring its total portfolio to 50 malls in Australia and New Zealand alone.

In addition, Westfield America holds a 99-year lease on the 427,000-square-foot shopping mall that stood in the underground shopping concourse of the World Trade Center in New York. (Westfield's lease further gave the company the right to expand the existing WTC mall up to 600,000 square feet.) When the new design was chosen to rebuild the World Trade Center, Westfield officially made its objections known to the Port Authority of New York and New Jersey, which owned the center.

Westfield's lease gives the firm the right to rebuild on the site or even expand its square footage, and the new design does call for 880,000 square feet of retail. The trouble is that in the old World Trade site, which was considered extremely profitable because of the thousands of commuters who trafficked the space, the bulk of the retail was on one level. In the new design by architect Daniel Libeskind, retail would weave over three or four levels.[12]

"We do not believe the retail portion of the design ultimately maximizes the ability for retailers and consumers to shop," says Peter Lowy. And it is a good shopping experience created by design, retailers, and management that makes a retail developer successful. (In September 2003 Westfield began discussions with the Port Authority of New York to sell its interest in the WTC retail net lease.)

"Unless you have a World Trade Center or something like that, from my business point of view, retail development is not as volatile as, say, the hotel or office sector," Peter Lowy says. "Every two months we do projections for every center so we see the trend well before it happens."

Peter Lowy adds, "Retail management is a very steady business that moves in increments, so if you see deterioration in your projections, you go in there and fix it. There should never be a situation where the cash flow suddenly drops and you didn't know it was going to happen."

THE MAVERICK APPROACH TO HIRING SAVVY MANAGERS

1. If you are merely a passive investor, hire active third-party managers to look over your property.
2. As a small real estate entrepreneur, you can do your own property management as long as you take the job seriously.
3. Your first priority should always be to take care of your tenants.
4. Remember, management consists of two parts: managing the property and managing the asset.
5. Standardize management procedures and adopt a reporting system.
6. High retention is a sign of management success.
7. Be flexible, adaptable, and attuned to local market changes.
8. Adopt a time management program.
9. Learn from the good and bad lessons of the past.
10. Maintain a comfortable environment for managers and building occupants.
11. As your company grows, be prepared to change your corporate management structure.
12. Integrate all parts of your company together for maximum efficiency.
13. Don't be afraid to do things differently.
14. Use strategies that have been successfully applied elsewhere.
15. Even if times get tough, stay the course.
16. Try to spot the next problem before it happens.

CHAPTER 10

Get Good Legal and Tax Counsel

Behind every Maverick stand good lawyers and tax advisors. Zoning laws, variances, land-use rules, and taxation regulations are all issues that can kill a well-conceived project. A competent advisory team will help you hold onto your most prized investments, even if things go decidedly wrong.

In a crowded New York conference room, a well-known real estate Maverick sits on one end of the table, flanked by a group of very impatient bankers on both sides. The Maverick, who happens to be Donald Trump, explains that he is in deep financial trouble. On top of that, he needs more capital from them—$65 million to be exact.

After everyone starts breathing again, Trump carefully explains that things are not as bad as they seem. This line of credit will simply give him enough room to work out the mess in which he, at the moment, has found himself.

He concludes the meeting by laying down the ultimate Trumpian line: "Look, I can tie you guys up for years—in court proceedings, bankruptcy filings, and the other legal maneuvers I'm good at—when forced."[1]

Trump knows how to effectively use the secret weapons that every successful real estate investor always keeps at the ready: tough lawyers and thorough accountants.

Real estate investors are inherent risk takers, entrepreneurs, and visionaries. Their focus is totally on the transaction, securing the property, or planning the next development. Someone has to come from behind to deal with zoning problems, contracts, forming syndications, arranging financing structures, pulling tax credits, and dealing with regulators. There is nothing simple about real estate, and the business gets more complicated every day.

Law firms specializing in real estate perform a number of essential, yet little known, functions. The Web site of one such national firm notes that its real estate attorneys "regularly represent national and regional lenders and borrowers in sophisticated real estate financings, ranging from traditional mortgage loan transactions to off-balance-sheet synthetic lease financings."

This is merely a small part of what this one firm does in regard to real estate law. Notice that it does not even mention many of the services required by a real estate investor who is in trouble and considering a bankruptcy filing, wanting to unwind a partnership, trying to arrange an asset-backed bond financing, interested in forming an investment fund, or needing to fend off a corporate takeover.

During Simon Property Group and Westfield America's hostile takeover bid of Taubman Centers, the battleground was mostly in the courts. In February 2003, as one of many examples, Taubman Centers filed a brief in the U.S. District Court in Detroit claiming that Simon made misleading assertions about the roles of Taubman's financial advisors. That brief was in reply to a brief filed a week earlier by Simon Property alleging numerous misdeeds by Taubman Centers.[2] When the crap starts flying in real estate, those who do the flinging are the lawyers.

Trump confronted his bankers by telling them that if he got the $65 million line of credit, he would end any thought of legal skirmishes. They ultimately agreed.

While there is always room for entrepreneurial players in the world of real estate investing, the environment today is not as wild and crazy as it has traditionally been. Those who grew their businesses in the loosely regulated climate of the post–World War II years have given way to the next generation of managers, many of whom are the children of those entrepreneurs. In this group are a strikingly large percentage of lawyers. Douglas Shorenstein and Richard LeFrak, both of whom succeeded their fathers in the family real estate business, are lawyers by education. At KB Home, Bruce Karatz, who followed founder Eli Broad into the leadership slot of the Los Angeles–based home builder, is also an attorney. This gives him a unique perspective that not all real estate Mavericks have.

LET ATTORNEYS DEAL WITH ZONING ISSUES

These days, with capital widely available for new construction, the biggest problem for the developer who has located a good piece of land is meeting all of the zoning and permit requirements. States and municipalities do not just automatically rubber-stamp new developments anymore. Therefore, it is a rare developer—or developer's attorney—who does not know his or her way around city hall.

Zoning problems are as a common as ants at a summer picnic. How does such a small thing as zoning get messy? Take this not-so-unusual case: A few years back, Home Depot wanted to build a store in Smithtown, New York, but the village was not so enamored of the retailer. The city's planning director asked the town board to amend the zoning ordinance, which would, in effect, block a Home Depot from being built. An attorney for Home Depot immediately responded by telling the board that if it amended the town code to block it, the company would file a lawsuit against the city.[3]

Threats of lawsuits are as common as requests for proposals, especially in big transactions.

READ THE SMALL PRINT

Zoning is merely one in a host of issues best dealt with by an attorney experienced in such matters. Lawyers should also be involved in reviewing every contract you are asked to sign. Wording has to be specific and inclusive. Besides, who but a lawyer can read these incomprehensively thick and verbose agreements?

KB Home, which began life as Kaufman & Broad in the late 1950s, has grown into a multi-billion-dollar company safely ensconced on both the S&P 500 and Fortune 500 lists. Among its 4,500 employees is a group of 15 lawyers, all of whom remain very busy at all times.

"We continue to build our in-house legal department," says Bruce Karatz, KB Home's chairman and chief executive officer. "We think it's a great training ground for people to eventually do other things in the company, and there is no substitute for having lawyers [on staff] who really love and buy into your business the way we do."

CONSIDER HIRING IN-HOUSE COUNSEL

Although KB Home can get good legal advice elsewhere, Karatz prefers having his team in-house. "You can always get a very fine lawyer, but then you are one of a dozen clients. They don't take our business, our customers, our product as seriously as we do."

Since legal issues and representation have become part and parcel of the real estate business, Karatz, who, as previously noted, is a lawyer himself, contends that a good legal education "is a tremendous background for this business."

Attorneys are just the first part of a necessary, professional team. Of equal importance are accountants. Again, for smaller entrepreneurs it is best to contract out these services. As your portfolio grows and ongoing concerns develop, however, you may want to consider bringing full-time professionals on board. There is almost no real estate transaction—purchase, sale, management, realignment, development—where accounting services are not needed.

It is not as though a brother-in-law or a friend of a friend will do; legal and accounting property issues can be extremely complex, and it is crucial to hire someone who specializes in these fields.

IT'S ALWAYS ABOUT TAXES

While an entrepreneur may be able to sniff out good properties and even negotiate advantageous deals, what happens to real estate in the area of taxes can make the difference between profit and loss.

Take something as endearing and ubiquitous as depreciation. The Internal Revenue Service defines depreciation very simply: When you buy a capital asset (a piece of equipment or a building for use in business), you expect to use that item for several years. The cost of these capital assets should be written off over the same period of time you expect the assets to earn income for you. Therefore, you must spread the cost over several tax years and deduct part of it each year as a business expense. As these assets (including properties) wear out, lose value, or become obsolete, you recover your cost as a business expense. This method of deducting the cost of business property is called *depreciation.*

Waxing rhapsodic about the importance of depreciation, Rainmaker Marketing Corporation of Houston claims that the true mission of real estate entrepreneurs is to uncover and benefit from the many available tax advantages offered by the IRS. As the firm puts it, "To defer tax consequences until another point in the future, while reaping significant financial rewards today, it only makes good business sense that commercial property owners obtain the highest possible depreciation expense allocations that are legally possible under the Tax Reform Act of 1986."[4]

The relationship between taxes and real estate is so important, the Tax Reform Act of 1986 was created to right what was perceived to be long-standing abuses of the real estate investment industry. By taking away key tax incentives, the act, one could argue, was a catalyst for the deep real estate recession that swept the industry in the late 1980s and early 1990s. The act had such severe consequences that the real estate lending industry collapsed, taking down most of the country's savings and loans with it.

As the *CPA Journal* noted in 1991, "The Tax Reform Act of 1986 has contributed to the decline of the real estate industry." It went on to list some of the myriad changes—elimination of capital gains tax differential, increased time period in regard to writing off taxes for depreciable real property, and limitation of deductions of passive investment losses—which contributed to the decline of the industry. "These changes have reduced the market value of real property, created an incentive for divesting real property, increased the difficulty of divesting real estate, and reduced the attractiveness of investing in new housing and construction."[5]

Although this all happened more than a decade ago, real estate, whether we like it or not, is still closely intertwined with the tax code. That's why it is extremely important to have smart, honest accountants on your team.

TAKE THE ROAD LESS TRAVELED

The history of successful real estate companies usually begins with a tale of some lanky, blue-collar son who decides to enter the construction trade and ends up—almost by accident but assuredly by sheer determination—building a huge real estate empire. One of the largest home builders in the country began on a different track. An accountant created the company, then it grew and achieved greatness under the stewardship of an attorney.

KB Home, one of the largest home builders in the United States and France, started modestly—almost on a whim. Thanks to good advice and counsel, along with well-timed moves, it has enjoyed enormous growth and success.

MEET THE MAVERICKS

Eli Broad

Birth Date: 1933

Occupation: Founder, Kaufman & Broad and SunAmerica, Los Angeles, CA

Education: BA, accounting, Michigan State University

Career Highlights:

- Cofounds home-builder Kaufman & Broad
- Moves Kaufman & Broad to southern California from Michigan
- Expands Kaufman & Broad to France
- Buys Sun Life Insurance
- Creates SunAmerica in 1993

Eli Broad graduated with honors from Michigan State University in 1954 with a degree in accounting and began working as an accountant. One of his early clients was a home builder in the Detroit area. "I was making about $75 a week after taxes, and I saw my client was making a lot of money. I said to myself, 'I could do that,' " he recalls.

Broad teamed up with his cousin, Donald Kaufman. With $25,000 of their own money, they started the home-building firm Kaufman & Broad in 1957.

"I was ripping to get into home building simply from an economic point of view," Broad says. "I needed to make money for my family."

Born in 1933, Broad is the son of Lithuanian immigrants who settled in Detroit. After graduating from college, he returned to Detroit, which was still enjoying a vibrant economy. With incomes rising, however, white families began to move out of the city into the new suburbs that were blossoming around the Motor City. Broad made his move into home building at the right time. According to one story, Kaufman & Broad's first housing division garnered $250,000 in sales on the first weekend of business and boasted $1.7 million in sales after the first year.[6]

Kaufman & Broad succeeded immediately because there was a demand for its product. It continued to succeed because, as an accountant, Broad kept an eye on financing. Instead of using traditional bank loans, he preferred lines of credit.

"You have to be conservative, you have to have reserves, and you have to have staying power," he insists. "You do not finance properties with short-term funds, no matter how low they are at the moment, because you do not know where interest rates will be in 18 months."

He adds, "While you must move aggressively in the market, you have to have a reasonable amount of equity and be fiscally conservative."

Broad not only had a sense of timing about his business, but he also had a wide view of the business. He realized the company's future would be limited if he stayed in Detroit, especially since the population was moving west. Kaufman & Broad tried Phoenix first, which was a big misstep. The company arrived just as the Arizona city, notorious for its boom-and-bust cycles, was heading into a recession. Gradually, Kaufman & Broad migrated even farther west, to southern California.

Always in search of long-term financing, Broad took his company public in 1961. A year later, it was the first home-building venture to be listed on the New York Stock Exchange.

In the early 1960s, Kaufman & Broad expanded rapidly into other states, mainly through acquisitions. In 1965, the company formed a mortgage subsidiary to arrange loans for its customers. Two years later, it became the first American home builder to start a development overseas when it began a project in France.

In 1971, Kaufman & Broad began building in Canada, and for the first time sales passed the $100 million mark.

Despite his success as a home builder, Broad was always a numbers person. It was the economics of home building that appealed to him, not the real estate itself. The problem with holding property, as he saw it, was that the real estate business was perceived to be very cyclical. So Broad looked around for a comparable business with more predictable earnings. He decided the company needed to branch into the insurance business. In 1971 he bought Sun Life Insurance. Over a 20-year period he built this into a major insurer called SunAmerica.

Broad is now in the corporate hall of fame for founding two Fortune 500 companies—KB Home (the current name of Kaufman & Broad) and SunAmerica (which was acquired by American International Group in 2001). But the building of these companies did not come overnight.

In 1986, Broad turned his attention to the insurance side of the business. He reorganized Kaufman & Broad into two separate firms: Broad, Inc. (later SunAmerica) was an insurance firm with Broad as its chairman and chief executive officer; and Kaufman & Broad Home, which was spun off to shareholders with Bruce Karatz as its longtime president and chief executive officer.

At that time, despite its reputation, Kaufman & Broad was still only a small company with revenues of $300 million. Its fortunes were about to change, though. Unlike Broad, Bruce Karatz was absolutely enamored of the real estate end of the business and had big plans for the company.

MEET THE MAVERICKS

Bruce Karatz

Birth Date: 1945

Occupation: Chairman and Chief Executive of KB Home, Los Angeles, CA

Education: BA, history, Boston University; JD, University of Southern California Law School

Career Highlights:

- Becomes chairman and chief executive of Kaufman & Broad
- Transforms Kaufman & Broad into KB Homes
- Buys Rayco, a San Antonio home builder
- Changes model home paradigm with KBnxt
- Leads KB Home to becoming a $5 billion company

Karatz, born in Chicago in 1945, was raised in Minneapolis. Upon completing high school, he moved east to college, getting a bachelor's degree from Boston University. After spending one Christmas in Los Angeles, with its palm trees blowing against a backdrop of blue skies, Karatz decided it was better to be in California than in Minneapolis during the winter and chose to go to law school at the University of Southern California.

Law degree in hand, Karatz went to work at a boutique law firm specializing in securities law. He stayed there for two years until a headhunter called about a job at a hot, young Los Angeles company called Kaufman & Broad. This was 1972, and Kaufman & Broad stock was selling at 50 times earnings.

Karatz didn't know anything about real estate or home building, but decided to take the job. He liked it so much, one day he asked Broad if he could be relieved of his attorney duties to actively take on an operations role within the company. The president acquiesced and Karatz was sent to Irvine, California, to be a land buyer and do entitlement work.

Two years later, Broad asked Karatz to take over a troubled assignment in Marseilles, France. While KB Home has grown to become one of the largest home builders in France, the company had a troubled start there. It moved to the Paris area in the late 1960s, but did not deliver a home until 1970. As Paris developments finally got under way, Kaufman & Broad expanded to other cities such as Marseilles. When Karatz took over in 1974, that division was floundering.

After two years in this business, Karatz still didn't know much about construction and he did not speak French. But he did have a great intuitive sense of what was needed in Marseilles—getting cooperation from the trade groups. He focused his efforts on key trades, making a point to be at the job site every morning at 7 A.M. to make sure everyone showed up when work was under way.

That first quarter in Marseilles, Kaufman & Broad delivered 75 homes, which was considered a huge number. Karatz was a hero. After two years, Karatz moved to Lyon, France, and then took over the company's primary French division in Paris. Karatz stayed in France for Kaufman & Broad for more than eight years, becoming the first American to be appointed director of France's National Federation of Builders and Developers.

KB Home still builds 4,000 homes a year in France. In 1985, the company acquired Bati-Service, a major French developer of affordable homes. In 2000, KB Home raised $117 million by taking half of its French subsidiary public, while retaining a controlling interest.

In the early 1980s, when Karatz returned from France to become president of what was then Kaufman & Broad Development Group, the housing business was rolling through a recession. The insurance business, on the other hand, was growing, and Eli Broad's focus was turning more and more in that direction. Where Broad went, so did the company's board. As a group, they were unhappy with the home-building business and even considered selling it.

Karatz met with Broad and convinced him to split the company, allowing him to take over the home-building side. Broad agreed and stayed on as chairman of Kaufman & Broad until 1992. (The current name, KB Home, was not unveiled until 2001.)

By the end of 2002, KB Home's U.S. division had operations in Arizona, California, Colorado, Nevada, New Mexico, and Texas. Although it tried to expand into other countries, the company has met with real success only in France and still owns a majority interest in Kaufman & Broad SA, which is traded on the ParisBourse exchange.

KB Home's primary market remains first-time and move-up home buyers, with the average home now selling for $190,000. Over the company's 45 year history, it has constructed more than 390,000 homes. It also owns a mortgage subsidiary called KB Home Mortgage Company.

GROW THROUGH ACQUISITIONS

In 2002, the company hit a milestone, surpassing $5 billion in revenue for the first time—an amazing advance considering that when Karatz took over the then-slumping home builder in 1986 it was doing just $300 million.

How Karatz came to erect a powerhouse in the home-building industry could eventually be a case study at his old alma mater across town, USC. Karatz moved aggressively to buy smaller operations, absorbed and expanded the better practices of these smaller companies, and wasn't afraid to change the traditional operations paradigm of the industry.

When Eli Broad began Kaufman & Broad, he was able to expand the company's reach by acquiring local builders instead of starting new operations from scratch. It was a lesson Karatz learned and expanded. Since 1996, KB Home has made 15 key acquisitions, including Dover/Ideal in Houston; PrideMark in Denver; Estes in Tucson; Lewis Homes, a major California developer and the number one builder in Las Vegas; Trademark Home Builders in Jacksonville, Florida; American Heritage Homes in Orlando; and Colony Homes, one of the largest private home builders in the Southeast, with operations in Atlanta, Raleigh, and Charlotte.

"Given that the top 10 home builders command only about 20 percent of the $200-billion-a-year U.S. new home market, we believe that further consolidation is in the cards for the industry," says Karatz. One widely reported study predicts the 20 largest home builders, which in 2002 held a 22 percent share of the new home market, would increase those numbers to 40 percent by 2010 largely through acquisitions.[7]

That is a good thing for consumers, Karatz maintains, as big, nationwide builders with superior supplier networks have the purchasing power to drive down the costs of building homes. National builders also have greater access to capital, and when they get the dollars, it is cheaper money. Since KB Home is national, it is also better protected against regional economic declines.[8]

USE BEST PRACTICES, EVEN IF THEY ARE NOT YOUR OWN

One of the most important companies Karatz acquired was San Antonio–based Rayco in 1996.

"Rayco had a 40 to 50 percent market share in San Antonio, which no other home builder ever had in a major market," Karatz explains. "It was an unbelievable kind of market share. I bought the company because not only was it a terrific business, but the principles under which they operated were sounder than mine."

What did Rayco do differently than the rest of the industry? It didn't construct speculative homes and then wait for customers to come and buy them. This had been the industry norm. Building specs got people into their dream homes quickly. Unfortunately, when the market turned, home builders were often left with large inventories of unsold homes—a very costly situation, because builders, not unlike retailers, usually end up selling off that inventory at deep discounts.

During the real estate recession of the early 1990s, home builders were sitting on an average nine-month supply of unsold homes; by 2002, the average supply dropped to four-months.[9]

Instead of building out a development, Rayco constructed its models to act as stores where potential buyers could pick and choose whatever accoutrements they wanted in their new homes (marble floors instead of tile, upgraded faucets, etc.).

"That old speculative home model was the same for the entire industry, and it lasted until 1996," says Karatz. Other home builders changed their paradigm as well, but Karatz claims it all started with KB Home once it acquired Rayco.

"When we open a community, we build our models. We don't build speculative homes. We wait until we have orders," Karatz shares. "You come in, give us a deposit, get preliminary mortgage approval, and then go to our studio and pick out all the options. We have 20,000 square feet of retail space that looks like a small Home Depot. Home buyers come in and select tile, bathtubs, faucets, barbecues, pools, and so on."

As the *Wall Street Journal* noted, "For years, people who wanted to differentiate their tract home from those down the block were often limited to several swatches of rug fabric or tile flooring on a salesperson's key ring. But, in an effort to find new sources of growth, many of the nation's biggest residential developers have begun to offer a bewildering array of options on everything from the type of marble in the entryway to the shape of the swimming pool."[10]

Until KB Home replicated what Rayco had done, "options for carpet samples were lined up in a corner and tile choices were either white or beige," jokes Karatz. "Choices were very limited."

KB Home's business model is called KBnxt. It does two things: reduces risk by not building speculatively and offers home buyers a customization option.

At KB Home Studios, buyers select the options and features they want, then roll the cost of these options into their monthly mortgage payment. Instead of buying a home and then running around trying to find the right carpet, window covering, and light fixtures, customers choose all that before construction.

"This process has allowed KB Home to give the power of choice directly to home buyers," says Karatz. The company allows buyers to select from among many floor plans and over 5,000 custom options at its KB Home Studios. All this is taken care of before KB Home breaks ground on a new home.[11] The cost of all these extras can then be tacked onto the mortgage taken out by the builder's own financing arm, KB Home Mortgage. It is true one-stop shopping.

For home buyers there is a good and a bad part to all of this. A stripped-down home costs less. However, home builders know that when customers have a chance to upgrade and make these improvements part of the overall mortgage, they will customize to their heart's content. That is good news for the home builders, because the margins from these options are better than the margins on the basic construction of the home.[12] It's also good for customers, because they get exactly what they want. The bad part for home buyers is that they wind up with higher monthly payments.

"We have a proprietary, risk-averse business model we call KBnxt that provides high earnings visibility and high margins, as well as the ability to sustain growth in most economic cycles," Karatz adds.[13]

CHANGE THE PARADIGM

The second way Karatz changed the home-building model was to computerize and improve the building processes. Traditionally, delivering houses on a fixed schedule was very difficult because it depended on the subcontracted crews to respond to a schedule that was haphazard at best. How well a particular site did in terms of meeting a deadline depended solely on the ability of that particular superintendent to get all parties to the development on time.

Frankly, Karatz says, the sites that built homes the fastest usually had superintendents who were the biggest jerks, constantly threatening the subcontracters that if they were not there they would not get their checks. "If you do a poor job of planning and make up for it by using a lot of four-letter words, and maybe steal contractors from another site, you still ended up being viewed as a terrific superintendent and you got a bonus to boot."

KB Home was able to ditch that inefficient system by computerizing the scheduling process. At its data center in Pomona, California, the company sends nightly scheduling e-mails to subcontractors and handles billings and payments.[14]

"With centralized scheduling, we have one or more persons who are responsible for getting a schedule out for all the homes being built in all our divisions," says Karatz. "As it happens, it's generally a woman who knows nothing about construction. She asks the trades how much advance time they will need to be notified when to be on site. If it's a week, they get a week reminder and then a reminder the day before. If they are a no-show, we cannot work with them."

The benefit to the subtrade is that KB Home can guarantee that when they show up, the site will be ready for them and they will not have to go home without working because the prior contractor did not get the job done.

"IT [information technology] is one of the competitive advantages we have over everyone else," says Karatz. "KB Home has one of the best computer-based scheduling programs I've seen," notes Matthew Moyer, an industry analyst for A.G. Edwards.[15] Karatz has found that, in today's environment, good technology advice is just as important as competent legal and accounting counsel.

FAVOR FORMAL STUDIES OVER INSTINCTS

Karatz may love the real estate business, but KB Home personnel are not allowed to fall in love with a piece of real estate. An entrepreneurial developer might wander upon a vast tract of land and instinctively conclude that it is a great place for a housing development. If the entrepreneur is right, he or she might make a fortune. If wrong, he or she could go broke.

KB Home tries to reduce its risk when it comes to new developments. Acquisition is a formal process. For starters, each division knows that no land can be acquired unless it has all entitlements in place. Next, each division has to prepare a book based on surveys and market studies. "We want to know the comps, what other people are doing, what the sales rates are, prices, surrounding architecture, and what it will cost," says Karatz. "We want to understand what the risks are."

This particular change was necessary because, while the industry often talked about margins, it never much considered the internal rate of return, which has value in commercial and industrial real estate, as well as in single-family-home building.

"The industry talked about what theoretical gross margins were," Karatz explains. "If the margins were 20 percent, we extrapolated that [it] meant we could get good profits. The problem with that was the results were not dependent on how quickly you could sell. Gross margins were only as good as the sales rates."

The new, relevant question is, how many homes per week are selling? "That is an entirely different question," Karatz observes. "It involves the concept of return on capital and the velocity at which you are turning those houses."

Obviously, like his predecessor Eli Broad, Karatz pays attention to the numbers. This includes a new look at the company's debt.

"It was always considered acceptable for home builders to have fairly high leverage, which allowed companies to go out and grow bigger than their capital would otherwise allow," says Karatz. "When times get tough, you take greater risk and people start figuring out that the industry would be better off less leveraged. And, of course, your returns increase when leverage goes down."

Karatz has done an admirable job of managing KB Home's debt. In 1992, when the company was doing $1 billion in revenue, it had 60 percent debt to total capitalization. When it reached the $5 billion mark, the debt-to-total-capitalization ratio was only 45 percent. (Historically, the industry's debt-to-capital ratio has been above 70 percent; by 2002 it dropped to below 50 percent.)[16]

There are other corporate numbers that turn people's heads. Perhaps, the one casual observers find most interesting is compensation. In 2002, the *Los Angeles Business Journal* reported that for the prior year Karatz's income totaled $44.5 million. In a city of overpaid entertainment executives, the *Journal* wryly reported, Karatz was the highest-paid executive in Los Angeles that year.

THE MAVERICK APPROACH TO GETTING GOOD LEGAL AND TAX COUNSEL

1. Always seek professional help for matters of law and accounting.
2. Let your lawyers deal with zoning and permit requirements.
3. Have every contract reviewed by an attorney.
4. Read the fine print closely.
5. If your real estate business grows sufficiently, consider hiring in-house legal and tax counsel.
6. Taxes are as important to real estate investment as appreciation potential.
7. Use best practices, even if they are developed elsewhere.
8. Sometimes it is better to grow through acquisition.
9. Rely on formal research—not just instincts—when making major investment decisions.
10. Harness the power of technology and use it to its full potential.
11. Avoid full build-out until the orders come in.

CHAPTER 11

Overcome Negative Responses

Expansion in the real estate business
often depends on an investor's ability to
overcome a "no" response. Remember,
a negative reaction is just a starting place.
After all, everyone has a point of weakness
and a drop-dead price.

Toward the middle of 2003, the country's shopping center bigwigs flashed their first-class tickets, settled in quietly for their flights to Las Vegas, and headed to the annual International Council of Shopping Centers spring convention. Anyone even tangentially involved in that end of the business was there.

Away from the hoi polloi, a couple of top guns sat around a table doing what they do every year—playing high-stakes poker. Not everyone is invited to the game. One rumor that came out of the session and rolled across the convention may not be true, but knowing the participants, everyone was willing to at least believe the veracity of the tale. Apparently, one of the players at the game was Robert Taubman, chief executive of Taubman Centers, a Bloomfield Hills, Michigan–based chain of 20 shopping malls throughout the United States. As he was sitting, studying his hand, Taubman's archnemesis, David Simon, quietly walked up behind him, leaned over, and whispered in his ear, "I see you are losing again."

Simon, chief executive officer of the Simon Property Group, had reason to be nasty. Simon Property, based in Indianapolis, ranks as the largest shopping mall chain in the United States. With 173 malls, Simon Property had wandered knee-deep into a bruising, ugly hostile takeover of the Taubman Centers. Weeks earlier, Simon Property won an important legal decision when a federal judge declared that the founding Taubman family couldn't use its 33.6 percent ownership stake to block Simon Property's $1.69 billion offer. Hence, the caustic nature of Simon's remark at the alleged poker game.

The battle was not over, as Taubman Centers declared it would appeal the decision because, the company claimed, "This ruling is so wrong that we are extremely confident that it will not withstand our appeal."[1]

Clearly, Taubman Centers was going to fight tooth and nail to stay independent, and it appeared that Simon Property was just as determined to force a takeover.

OVERCOMING NEGATIVE RESPONSES TAKES AN ARRAY OF TOOLS

Expansion in the real estate business, as elsewhere, often depends on the ability to overcome the "no." A negative response could come from anywhere: a city that doesn't want to create zoning for a new development, a neighborhood that doesn't want what you seek to build, the owner of a building who doesn't want to sell out, or a company protecting a portfolio of properties you really want to get your hands around.

To get past these negative responses requires using all of the implements in your box of tricks—from the concrete and solid offer to the going-ballistic response, from the patient wining and dining of a prospective customer to the calling of the lawyers.

There is no singular trait shared by all of the real estate Mavericks, but they are often patient, very determined, and not afraid to strong-arm the decision-making process.

That is one of the reasons why the Simon-Taubman battle was so interesting. Simon Property Group unsuccessfully attempted a number of approaches to get around Taubman Centers defenses. Finally, it just kept raising the stakes, bringing on the lawyers, and elevating the level of animosity.

Taubman Centers itself was created by a true Maverick—Alfred Taubman—who built the company and then passed the stewardship to his son Robert Taubman. For a while, Alfred Taubman amused himself by becoming chairman of Sotheby Holdings, the famed auction house of fine art. But that proved to be a disaster when he was convicted of price-fixing and sent to jail.

The Taubman family and supporters bitterly complained that the Simon Group pounced while Alfred Taubman sat in a prison cell in Rochester, Minnesota, unable to fight back.[2]

Simon Property Group denies it, but who is to say that this was not, in fact, a calculated tactic in what has become a messy battle. The Simon story is that David Simon had wanted to buy the much smaller Taubman Centers for a couple of years and kept the overtures friendly, but was always rebuffed.

GO HOSTILE

The *Wall Street Journal* reported the battle of the shopping mall titans this way: "In a belligerent, expletive laced diatribe, David Simon told Robert Taubman that resistance was a bad idea. In sworn testimony, Taubman said Simon reminded him that his father was in jail and then asked, "How was [that] going to look in a takeover battle?"[3]

Simon, of course, disputes being belligerent, but what the heck, why not? It has always been a useful, if not a last-ditch tactic to win in contentious bargaining. Granted, it is a somewhat pitiful maneuver, but businesspeople never have ceased and probably never will cease to use it as a ploy. Not everyone can use the threat and the scary delivery of the threat credibly, because they do not have the personality for it and often they don't have the assets to make good on those threats.

There is always the bluff, but if the bluff is called, it is like taking three steps backward, and the bargaining position becomes worthless.

Simon Property, being one of the biggest real estate investment trusts in the United States, certainly had the assets, and it had been through a number of large takeovers in the past. While the struggle with Taubman represented the first hostile bid among major companies in the REIT business, it is probably equally true that earlier takeovers were not exactly friendly and that the targets were offered deals they could not refuse.

It was not just Simon Property. Frank Lowy led his company, Westfield America, in a hostile takeover of Rodamco North America NV in 2001. Netherlands-based Rodamco itself became one of the largest owners of regional shopping centers in the United States after its takeover of Chicago-based Urban Shopping Centers in 2000.[4]

Lowy started the onslaught on a reluctant Rodamco by acquiring a 23.9 percent stake in the company. That allowed it to launch a proxy fight for control.

TAKE THE ARGUMENT PUBLIC

Both as an acquisition tactic and as a defense, it is often a good maneuver to present the transaction to the public via the media or to shareholders through corporate communications. Donald Trump boasted that he was able to gain leverage in one of his early deals by leaking a potentially damaging report to the press.

Swaying public opinion or shareholders is certainly a valid and time-honored way to create a stronger negotiating position. Politicians do it, and so do savvy businesspeople. And it cuts both ways. In the Rodamco-Westfield fight, Gerald Egan, who was Rodamco's chief executive at the time, wrote to his shareholders accusing Westfield of self-serving plans to gain control of the portfolio in order to collect massive management fees. Westfield countered in the press, saying "the interests of Westfield Management are strongly aligned with those of all shareholders in Rodamco."[5]

In the Simon-Taubman fight, David Simon simultaneously sent a formal letter to Taubman's board in regard to a takeover offer and issued a news release to the press on November 13, 2002.[6]

David Simon quickly moved on the shareholders in February

2003, getting 85 percent of the Taubman shareholders to support the bid. The Taubman family and other interests owned a controlling stake in the company through a type of stock known as Series B.[7]

BRING IN A PARTNER

As entrepreneurial investors begin to build a portfolio of properties, the next deal, whatever it may be—a small shopping center at the edge of town or two apartment communities in the next village— usually ends up being slightly bigger than the one before. That means taking on a little more risk, which becomes even more heightened when the owners of the desired property say no.

Other than patience, all tactics in a less-than-friendly transaction require some expense. Certainly this is true if attorneys have to be brought into the battle. One way to moderate the added expense, while at the same time adding some weight to your side of the battle, is to bring in a partner.

Yes, the total 36-shopping-mall portfolio of Rodamco was mighty tempting, but Frank Lowy knew he could cut his risk and add some significant power behind his offer by letting others take some of the deal. In the end, Rodamco agreed to be sold for $5.3 billion (including assumption of debt) to a powerhouse tag team of Westfield, Simon Property, and the Rouse Company. Simon Property returned the favor, bringing to the Taubman fight a co-bidder, Westfield America.

GET AHEAD OF THE HOSTILITY

There are a few things that can be done if you know that you will be heading into a situation where the seller is going to be reluctant to deal. The best tactic is to offer a fair, if not generous, price. A low bid is insulting and will likely make a potentially bad situation worse. A fair to generous bid at least gets the other party thinking. If the potential acquiree comes back with an alternative offer that is not too outrageous, you know you have gotten the game started—and that is where you want to be.

It is also important to do your homework, so that once you get the other party's attention, you can back up your bid. You must understand as well as possible the value of the property or properties that you are targeting. Again, you do not want to insult the seller when heading into potentially turbulent waters, so try to figure out the other side's priorities. Negotiating experts say that knowing the most important issues—other than for them to hold onto their properties—can help you avoid pushing too hard on the sensitive ones.[8]

Sometimes when acquiring other companies, the future employment of the people in the other organization is a sticking point. In such cases, at some level in the discussion you may want to offer to keep key personnel. When Simon Property acquired DeBartolo Realty Corporation in 1996, it kept an important player, Richard Sokolov. In 1982, Sokolov joined DeBartolo and eventually climbed to the position of president and CEO. When Sokolov moved to Simon he became president and chief operating officer.

Also, the principal personnel of the target company may be near retirement age and looking for security without a tax problem, meaning a generous offer of minority interest in your company could be the ticket to completing a deal.

"Most acquirees are going to have a tax issue, so they would rather have partnership units in the acquiring company," explains Richard Moore, a REIT analyst with McDonald Investments in Cleveland. "For example, when CBL & Associates Properties bought the Richard E. Jacobs Group portfolio, Richard Jacobs was ready to sell. He was getting on in years and didn't have a management succession team. When he sold, he ended up with a boatload of CBL stock—12 million shares—in the form of units. He got a dividend and future prospects in CBL."

In real estate, an unwanted suitor can pose unusual difficulties because of the enormous tax problems. The best way to sell out is into an operating partnership (OP), which is the way most REITs are structured. If an owner sells into the OP, it is not a taxable event because the acquiree takes back OP units in the exchange. The acquiree then collects dividends on the OP units just as if they were stock, but the dividends aren't taxable. An acquiree can only hope that when forced to make a deal, it is going to be with a company that is organized as an OP. More opposition would definitely occur if the company bearing down on the acquisition was in some way troubled and the future outlook not so sanguine.

How did it work out for Richard Jacobs? When the deal concluded in 2002, CBL stock was at $25. By 2003 the stock was trading at $44. For Jacobs, it was in his best interest to find the right REIT—a company that was going to grow and make his properties grow, thus pushing up his newfound stock.

BE PATIENT

Winning over a reluctant seller takes time, whether the approach is subtle or hostile. Maverick investors can always refer to an acquisition that took one or two years to complete, not because the deal was tricky, but because it took that long for the target to sell. AMB Corporation, the San Francisco–based industrial REIT, once set its sights on two buildings at John F. Kennedy International Airport in New York. The buildings were finally acquired two years later.

Hamid Moghadam, chief executive of AMB, opted for a benign approach, knowing that the owner of these two buildings did not have to sell and would prefer to keep the properties. Moghadam's tactic was to let the owner know he was interested in two of his properties, maintain good relations with the owner, and, when appropriate, remind the owner he was still interested if and when he thought of selling.

Here is something to keep in mind: If you don't succeed on your first try, more often than not you will get a second chance.

Back in 1996, one of Sam Zell's companies, Manufactured Home Communities, entered into a bruising hostile takeover of Chateau Communities only to be rebuffed when the target was nearly in his grasp. In 2003, Zell turned his attention on Chateau again. This time it looked like he would get what he wanted.

Chicago-based Manufactured Housing is one of the smaller REITs that Sam Zell founded and for which he now serves as chairman of the board. The company owns and operates manufactured housing communities, as does Chateau Communities. Sales for Manufactured Housing total just under $300 million.

The 1996, Chateau stymied Manufactured Housing's hostile takeover by the preponderance of insider ownership in regard to OP units, enough of which were converted to common shares at the eleventh hour to prevent Zell from acquiring control.[9]

Seven years later, Zell again looked at Chateau and saw it was in weaker financial condition and under the stewardship of a new CEO. Suddenly, Manufactured Home's $1.8 billion bid did not look so bad.

A seven-year wait is a bit extreme, but if at first you don't succeed . . .

BRING IN THE LAWYERS AND THE ACCOUNTANTS

At some point in the pursuit of a reluctant suitor it will be time to call in the attorneys, who bring some value-added services to the deal beyond framing contracts. If litigation occurs (in bigger hostile takeovers that always happens), the attorneys will handle valuation testimony and analysis, strategic planning in case formulation, and presentation.

The heart of the Simon-Taubman conflict was a lawsuit taking aim at Taubman family control. That lawsuit revealed in court proceedings that during a 1998 restructuring, the family hired its own team of advisers, including the law firm of Wachtell Lipton Rosen & Katz, pitting it against shareholders and institutional partners. According to a document from the proceedings, the goal of the restructuring was to boost the family's power over the REIT to avoid a shareholder vote on a corporate overhaul. Taubman claims the purpose of the 1998 restructuring was to allow large institutional investors to unwind their investments.[10]

One of the purposes of Simon's lawsuit clearly was to bring all the back dealing to the public's and shareholders' attention.

If the newspapers cover the deal, your attorneys can always become your mouthpiece, even if they only say, "Due to the nature of the transaction, my client cannot speak to the press at this moment."

With lawyers come accountants, not so much to work the numbers on the target property, but to work the tax angle. As noted, real estate and tax issues go hand in hand.

In 2002, Oak Brook, Illinois–based Inland Group sold one of its properties, Shorecrest Shopping Center in Racine, Wisconsin, for $6.2 million. It then took that money, plus another $7.3 million, and bought a much larger property called Deer Trace in Kohler, Wisconsin. What made the deal possible was something called a *1031 exchange,* a method of swapping the value of one property to buy into another that, unlike an outright sale, defers capital gains taxes. These 1031 exchanges are one of the few remaining real estate tax shelters.[11]

While companies like Inland Group use 1031 exchanges to swap older properties for new, back in the 1990s aggressive aggregators like Simon Property Group used 1031 exchanges to build their portfolios. Among the Simon Property deals exploiting the 1031 exchange were its acquisitions of Edward J. DeBartolo Corporation and New England Development.[12]

ACQUISITIONS CAN DEFINE A CORPORATE STRATEGY

Melvin Simon, born in 1926, and Herbert Simon, born in 1934, grew up in New York and later attended City College of New York. After a stint in the armed services, Mel Simon stayed in Indianapolis, initially working as a leasing agent. When he became interested in forming his own company, younger brother Herbert joined him in Indianapolis, along with a third brother, Fred Simon (who resigned in 1983 to pursue other interests). The year was 1960, and the newly minted Melvin Simon & Associates opened its first fully owned shopping center, Southgate Plaza, in Bloomington, Indiana.

Strip-center development was the company's first line of business. It stayed with those projects for a few years before moving on to bigger things, opening its first enclosed mall—the University Mall in Fort Collins, Colorado—in 1964. That was a busy year for the company. It also opened Mounds Mall in Anderson, Indiana, and College Mall in Bloomington, Indiana, in 1964.

New development proceeded at such a quick pace that by the end of 1967, Melvin Simon & Associates was opening new facilities at a rate of more than 1 million square feet annually. By 1967, the quick-growing company owned more than 3 million square feet of retail space.

Except for some organizational changes (Mel Simon became chairman and Herbert Simon president of Melvin Simon & Associates)

MEET THE MAVERICKS

Melvin Simon

Birth Date: 1926

Occupation: Cochairman of Simon Property Group; co-owner of the Indiana Pacers, Indianapolis, IN

Education: BS, accounting, City College of New York; MBA (emphasis on real estate), City College of New York

Career Highlights:

- Forms Melvin Simon & Associates (with brothers Herbert and Fred)
- Builds first enclosed malls in 1964
- Builds the Forum Shops at Caesar's Palace in Las Vegas
- Builds the Mall of America in Bloomington, Minnesota
- Forms Simon Property Group and issues initial public offering

and slightly larger projects (it opened Towne East Square in Wichita, Kansas, its first enclosed mall of more than 1 million square feet), the company proceeded through the first three decades building retail wherever opportunities arose, anywhere in the country.

In 1990 things began to change for the company. David Simon, son of Mel Simon, joined as executive vice president and chief financial officer. Five years later he became president and chief executive officer of the company, and Mel and Herbert Simon became cochairmen.

MEET THE MAVERICKS

David Simon

Birth Date: 1961
Occupation: Chief Executive Officer of Simon Property Group, Indianapolis, IN
Education: BS, Indiana University; MBA, Columbia University
Career Highlights:
- Merges firm with DeBartolo, Corporate Property Investors
- In a joint venture, acquires 10 regional malls from New England Development
- With two partners, completes takeover of Rodamco
- Enters into acrimonious takeover battle of Taubman Centers

David Simon, who was born in 1961, received his undergraduate degree from Indiana University, followed by an MBA from Columbia University. He worked as an associate at First Boston and became a vice president with Wasserstein Perella before joining his father's company.

David Simon apparently inherited his aggressive genes from his father and uncle. His appearance in the family firm coincided with some massive corporate changes. First, however, came two of the most grandiose retail projects in the country, both of which have since only increased in stature and reputation.

In 1992, Melvin Simon & Associates opened the Forum Shops at Caesars (the huge casino and hotel in Las Vegas), which to this day remains the most successful mall in the country based on sales per square foot. That same year, the company hit another milestone, opening the Mall of America in Bloomington, Minnesota, the largest enclosed shopping and entertainment complex in the United States.

Just one year later, Simon Property Group was formed when the old family firm went public in what at the time was the largest REIT initial public offering in history. In 1995, David Simon was elevated to his current titles.

The company's first major acquisition came in 1996 when it merged with DeBartolo. That deal added 49 regional malls, 11 community shopping centers, and a mixed-use property to the company's portfolio, making it the largest REIT in the country. For a couple of years it also sported a new name: Simon DeBartolo Group.

The corporate vision changed when Simon Property went public in 1993. Before then, the company was known primarily as a developer. Post-1993, as the regional mall business matured in the country such that a lot of new malls did not need to be built, the focus shifted to ownership and generating a larger market share.[13]

In the years following the IPO, according to one Simon executive, the company initiated a strategy that involved both consolidation and partnerships. Fed by mergers and acquisitions, the company seemed as though it could not buy enough.[14]

HOSTILE TAKEOVERS CAN BE FRIENDLY

Were these mergers all friendly, starting with the DeBartolo deal? "There could have been some hostilities, but in the end both sides saw it as an opportunity to get bigger," notes Moore. "The current chief operating officer is an old DeBartolo guy, but I don't think you are going to see any Taubman guys joining Simon if that merger happens."

"Nobody likes being taken over," Moore adds. "And so, while Simon's takeovers may have begun not quite on a completely friendly note, they always ended up making business sense. That is one of the things the Simons shake their heads about on the Taubman mess, because in the acquisitions of Corporate Property Investors [1998], New England Development [1999], and Rodamco [2001], the acquirees could have put up a bigger fight. They really didn't cherish being taken over, but in the end they looked at the deals being offered and decided it was a business proposition that was too good to pass up."

It could be said that at the time of the mergers, Simon paid an excessive price for Corporate Property Investors and New England Development. But Moore points out that the deals have turned out well.

DEALS MUST BE ABOUT MORE THAN JUST GETTING BIGGER

When asked about the Simon-Taubman merger fight, Ross Smotrich, a REIT analyst with Bear Stearns in New York, explains that it should not be taken as an isolated event. What you have to do, he suggests, is look at the evolution of the shopping mall industry to see why Simon Property Group made the moves it did. In many respects, the mall business is the classic mature industry, one in which size and market share matters.

By some estimates there were 2,000 malls in the country in 1998. Five years later that number had shrunk to 1,500. Sometime over the next few years those numbers could drop even more, probably to about 1,200—and of that amount, investors will care only about the most productive malls (higher sales per square foot), or approximately two-thirds of the total.

"The original premise of the mall," Smotrich continues, "is that the large department store anchors acted as destinations, around which you build in-line shops. Anchors draw the people, who end up supporting the specialty retailer like the Gap or The Limited. This concept, however, has evolved. So, in order to remain competitive, the malls have to change, which often implies remerchandizing, which in turn can be expensive. Those malls that don't remain competitive become obsolete."

The third consideration, Smotrich adds, is the slower pace of new mall development. Historically, mall development was predicated on buying large pieces of land on the outskirts of civilization and then waiting for the population to catch up. As the population grew, the developer would essentially give pads to the anchors, sell off the outlying parcels to fast-food chains and auto dealers, and retain the in-line shops for the in-house account. That is not taking place anymore. It has become difficult to find those large tracts of land, anchors are more focused on current sales, population growth patterns are often not so predictable, and, for some cities, there has been a population movement back into the city itself. The result has been a decline in mall development. Between 2003 and 2008, only about 40 regional malls are expected to be constructed, a growth rate of only around 1.5 percent.

"In the context of all that, Simon Property's goal since it went public is to upgrade the quality of its mall portfolio," says Smotrich. "That means selling off the less productive malls and controlling more of the productive malls—and Taubman centers are among the most productive malls in the country."

Over time, Smotrich continues, if Simon increases the average quality of its asset base in terms of productivity—sales per square foot—and at the same time builds a greater overall market share, the company will have better leverage with retailers.

David Simon would not disagree with that analysis. "Our goal is to maintain our position as a leading company in our industry and to continue to increase shareholder value," he says. "This will be achieved by focusing on those strengths that made us an industry leader, by divesting ourselves of assets that do not create value for our portfolio, and by continuing to develop ways to connect in a meaningful way with the customer."[15]

Retail real estate is slightly different from other property sectors in that many independent companies operate within the individual properties, and those same independent companies will often be tenants at numerous similar properties. As retail real estate companies get bigger, they can encourage tenants to consider locating across a wider portfolio of properties. This creates leverage. If you own a single mall, it is either appealing to a store like the Gap or it is not. That is the end of the conversation. A company like Simon, which owns properties in 25 of North America's largest cities, can say to the Gap, "You want to be in my beautiful property in Atlanta, right? How about helping me out with this other property as well? The leverage—or horse trading, depending on your point of view— becomes greater as the portfolio of retail properties becomes bigger. With higher-quality properties, the leverage becomes even more heightened.

If Simon Property takes over another company—and inherits a new portfolio—its objective would be to upgrade the acquisitions to the level of its older properties. If malls in the new portfolios are missing key retailers, with Simon Property's weight, it can suggest to those retailers that they should be tenants in its newer malls as well. These retailers would certainly take a serious look at the suggestion.

HOSTILE ACTIONS ARE DIFFICULT

It is always best to avoid an overly aggressive move against a target, whether it is a small strip mall owned by a friend of a friend or a portfolio of industrial properties accumulated by a local developer. Moving against private owners is extremely chancy, because they can just say no. If they do, what recourse is left, unless you have some leverage or knowledge of the target's financial position?

When the target is a public company, a whole new set of parameters exists. Since shareholders have a say in the proposal, hostile or otherwise, anything can basically happen. Even so, as the Simon-Taubman brawl shows, hostile actions can be nettlesome at best.

"In order to do merger and acquisition action in the REIT space," says Smotrich, "you have to have the alignment of the moon and stars. Hostile takeovers are difficult. There are so many takeover defenses built into individual REITs that hostile actions are challenging, which is the reason there have not been too many hostile takeovers that work. In fact, there have not been too many hostile takeovers that actually happened."

BREAK NEW GROUND

Simon Property Group specializes in enclosed mall and related retail properties, operating in all phases of the business, including asset and property management. It is also involved in leasing and tenant relations, financial reporting and analysis, acquisition, construction, and development. As of 2003, the company owned and had an interest in 243 properties encompassing an aggregate of 183 million square feet of gross leasable area in 36 states. The company further owns or has interests in eight additional assets in Europe and Canada.

In 1999, the company launched a campaign to brand its malls. It is also one of the few REITs to have shares included on the Standard and Poor's 500 Index.

When asked to define his company, David Simon responded by saying, "disciplined, focused, resilient, ambitious, innovative."[16]

Simon Property targets larger malls, typically located in more affluent areas, and is willing to pay relatively high prices in order secure properties in such locations, reports brokerage firm Stifel Nicolaus in St. Louis. "Simon Property's size offers it a significant advantage when compared to its peers in the sector, as its lower cost of capital and large portfolio provide it with advantages in competing for acquisitions in the market."[17]

With a market capitalization in excess of $6 million, it is the largest mall REIT, Stifel Nicolaus continues. "Further, its cost of debt and equity is lower than most other REITs, allowing it to make acquisitions accretively that other companies cannot. With its current hostile bid for Taubman Centers, it has blazed a trail by initiating the first major hostile takeover bid in the REIT sector."[18]

Even if Simon's bid fails, the Simon-Taubman fight dispels the myth that some REITs are impenetrable, comments Bob Steers, co-portfolio manager at Cohen & Steers Capital Management.[19]

As David Simon obviously observed, Taubman Centers had been trading at a discount to its peers in the mall sector, as returns on some of its mall developments were shallower than expected. What Simon saw when he made his bid was a company that, after a five-mall building spree, had two of the new properties performing below expectation. At the same time, the family patriarch was in prison. And while shares of other retail REITs posted gains of about 12 percent over the previous nine months, Taubman Centers shares had fallen 5 percent.[20]

"REITs with large family block positions could become targets if their stocks are trading at deep enough discounts," Steers says.[21]

The Simon-Taubman skirmish dented the feeling of immunity previously enjoyed by some families who hold major blocks of shares in REITs, says Matt Lustig, a managing director of real estate investment banking at Lazard Freres. The end result, Lustig adds, is that REITs will likely be more open to a takeover offer. "There's a feeling that a board's time and reputation are on the line when defending against a hostile deal, which companies may want to avoid," he says.[22]

If a hostile takeover breaks new ground, that is fine with David Simon. It just makes it easier for the next acquisition.

David Simon says his company's mission, "is to be the leading developer, owner and manager of retail real estate in North America through the creation and continual enhancement of shareholder value in a high-quality portfolio of premier properties."[23]

To which Moore concludes, "The Simons have a tendency to get what they want."

Perhaps not. In October 2003, Michigan's governor signed a law that, in effect, blocked a takeover of the locally based Taubman Centers. As a result, Simon and Westfield withdrew their offer for the company.

THE MAVERICK APPROACH TO OVERCOMING NEGATIVE RESPONSES

1. Don't be afraid to use all of the negotiating tools at your disposal to get what you want.
2. Resort to hostile measures if you have no other option.
3. Air your squabble in public if necessary to sway public opinion and bring more sympathy to your side.
4. Bring in a partner if it will help to get the deal done.
5. Try to head off any expected hostility before it starts.
6. Be patient. Hostile deals take time.
7. Be ready to bring out the big guns, namely, your attorneys and accountants.
8. Turn a hostile takeover into a friendly one if you possibly can.
9. Even hostile deals must make strategic sense. Otherwise, they can damage your business and your reputation.
10. Unwelcome actions are risky and difficult to execute successfully.
11. If necessary, break new ground.

CHAPTER 12

Sell to Your Advantage

When investing in real estate, the acquisition of property is just the start of a long process. Somewhere down the line, that property will have to be sold. You must make sure the sale is done under the right conditions to book a profit. This is a feat that even the best investors don't always get right.

Paul Reichmann remains one of the most enigmatic figures in recent North American real estate history. In the 1980s, he and his brother Albert built the world's largest real estate company, Olympia & York Development, with an estimated value of $10 billion, only to see it disappear in one of the greatest business flameouts on either side of the Atlantic Ocean.

In May 1992, Olympia & York filed for bankruptcy court protection, having by some estimates more than $20 billion in debt.

Ostensibly, the main cause of the bankruptcy filing—the largest in Canadian history—was a massive, multi-billion-dollar development called Canary Wharf that Olympia & York was constructing in London. Eventually, it became a very successful enterprise under the stewardship of Paul Reichmann, but in its early days, Olympia & York attempted the most difficult of tasks: constructing a hugely expensive project in the throes of a severe recession that stretched from the United States to Canada to London and the rest of Europe. As Canary Wharf's buildings were rising, so were vacancies in new and old projects in all of the big financial cities throughout North America and Europe.

There were, of course, other financial and structural problems with Olympia & York, as well as with the management style of Paul Reichmann. No one doubts Reichmann is an extremely astute businessman, but even the best have flaws, and in the world of real estate, Reichmann suffered a serious management shortcoming: not being able to let go of anything he owned. Even in the face of a coming recession and debt difficulties he refused to sell one building in the vast Olympia & York portfolio.

In his book, *The Reichmanns,* Anthony Bianco summed up Paul Reichmann's supreme investment weakness in this manner: "Reichmann's aversion to selling, which in the end would be revealed as one of his greatest deficiencies as a businessman, ran so deep that it seemed encoded in his very genes."[1]

As difficult as it is to acquire real estate under the right conditions, it is often just as hard to sell under optimal conditions for making a hefty profit on the investment.

THINK ABOUT SELLING WHEN TIMES ARE GOOD

The most popular cliché in regard to real estate remains "location, location, location." However, a second, equally overused maxim, holds a lot of truth: "The best time to sell is when you don't have to."

It sounds simple, but this advice is usually ignored. The rationale smacks of logic: It is best to make a sale when there is no pressure to do so, which means you can wait for your price and make the deal on terms you deem appropriate for both you and the buyer.

This is a difficult lesson to learn in real estate. After all, in the tradition of Maverick Sam Zell, many investors are focused on accumulating properties under the notion that bigger is better. Still, even the largest companies have had to learn the benefits of strategic divesting.

"Despite having a very strong attitude toward long-term ownership," notes Jeffrey Hines, president of Hines in Houston, "in the mid-1980s, we saw the market was entering a confluence of weakening demand and very strong capital flows [easy financing for new construction], so we did, in fact, sell five or six projects and built a strong capital position." It was a ripe time to sell. The panic unloading of real estate was still a few years away.

With its healthier capital structure, Hines made it through the tough real estate recession of the late 1980s and early 1990s, but it was not easy. Jeffrey Hines still wistfully notes, "I wish we had sold a few more buildings."

Paul Reichmann, who was born in 1930, is slightly younger than the first generation of real estate Mavericks you have met in this book, such as Walter Shorenstein, Sam LeFrak, Gerald Hines, and Dick Dusseldorp, all of whom scored well in the postwar decades of the 1960s and 1970s. Yet, like them, Reichmann's inclination was always to hold onto what he had wrought.

It really took some members of the second generation to change this type of thinking. Up until 1990, the Shorenstein Company never made a sale. Like other companies, such as Olympia & York, it realized a bit too late that there is always a time for letting go.

"The recession in 1990 was our first experience with declining real estate values, and we decided when the market turned strong again, it would be better to sell. As a result, when the economy slowed down again at the new millennium [just a decade later] we were in position to buy when others needed to sell," says Douglas Shorenstein, chairman and chief executive of the eponymous company. "And that has been our strategy."

SELL WHEN THE PROPERTY IS AT THE TOP OF ITS GAME

Shorenstein Company still holds onto properties, but it has since become a very active seller. "Because we are constantly in the market to buy, we know what values are on the sell side," Shorenstein notes. "If we've added all the value we can to a property, if the building is leased, and capital is flowing hellaciously, we will sell because there is nothing more we can do. We will sell if we can get a profit."

For real estate investors, the goal is to bring any particular property to the top of its performance potential, then sell into the market to get maximum pricing. The key is the readiness of the property itself, combined with the readiness of the market. In a perfect world, you would have both.

"Most of the assets in our portfolio have a flaw," observes John Kukral, president and chief executive officer of Blackstone Real Estate Group, the New York–based opportunity fund. "They are underleased, need rehabilitation, have a major tenant who is rolling over, or in one way or another need extensive asset management." Kukral's objective is to fix any flaws in the property, and once it is in pristine shape, to sell.[2]

Different markets attract different investment interest at different times. Sometimes San Francisco has a lot of capital flowing into it, other times it is Washington, D.C. You have to understand the market and the capital flows, because there are different sources of capital—pension funds, REITs, even foreign investors—each with varied needs and requirements.

"We buy an asset, stabilize it, and create cash flow," Shorenstein shares. "Usually that means a 10 percent current return. If we can add another 5 to 7 percent [thanks to a willing buyer], we will sell it. If the market will give it to us, we will take it."

TRY FOR THE CYCLE TOP

At the end of 1997, Kukral recognized that a significant part of its portfolio included properties in which the asset management and rehabilitation function had been completed. When he saw the prices being paid for assets at the time, Kukral felt it was right to sell from both an asset management and capital markets perspective. Between April and December 1998, he sold $3.2 billion in assets representing 26 different properties.[3]

John Hirschfeld, then managing director of Eastdil Realty, was looking over the real estate market in 2001 and noted how positive the signs were for deal making. "Now is a good time to sell because companies can net high proceeds and at the same time lock in low, long-term rent."[4] When asked how long the window of opportunity would last, Hirschfeld summed up the downside for those investors who just could not let go. "Waiting to sell could increase the possibility that real estate value will decline and/or long-term interest rates, which affect occupancy, will rise."[5]

SELL STRATEGICALLY

In the late 1990s, at the top of the tech bubble, vast amounts of capital were sucked out of other economic sectors to feed the flow of technology companies that were coming to market. After the halcyon days of the mid-1990s, the REIT sector found itself devoid of Wall Street interest and capital. Without the ability to raise dollars, the days of REITs as serial acquirers dimmed. This forced break from their own frenzy of acquisition gave companies time to rethink their portfolios and weed out those properties that were not throwing off the needed rates of return.

If the time to sell is ripe, figure out which properties are most important to the bottom line and trim the rest from your portfolio. Also, figure out which properties are strategically important to going forward, so that any sale benefits your overall strategy.

CONSIDER ALL INQUIRIES

It is not unusual for property owners to receive unsolicited and unexpected inquiries about a property that is not considered to be for sale. The first response is always to dismiss these queries. But the better part of valor is to listen to the offer. Sometimes buyers have a proposition that is difficult to turn down.

Remember, even if the offer is not exactly to your liking, keep the relationship friendly, because at some point in the future, the potential buyer may come back with a deal that is more interesting. Alternatively, if your situation turns bleak and you need to raise money, you will know where to find a willing buyer.

So say no to offers you are not interested in at the moment, but not with total finality.

In 2001, Beacon Capital Partners decided to sell its Technology Square complex in Cambridge, Massachusetts, to the Massachusetts Institute of Technology for $278.8 million. On a square-footage basis, the deal came in at a hefty $240 a square foot—a terrific sum for the seller, which did not have the property on the market, but decided to seek a buyer only after, as the company reported, "a number of unsolicited inquiries made about the property prompted Beacon to consider selling."[6]

OFFER SOMETHING BACK

Not everyone will want your property at the price you hope to receive, which means you might have to compromise. When trying to hold the line on pricing, you can be flexible on financing and the terms for such financing. You have to figure out what you want most—the price or the terms of the deal. In many negotiations, one or the other has to give.

It also helps to be creative in your deal making. Perhaps selling a package of properties would work better, or you can do a part-sale, part-trade transaction.

When Hines put the 1.8-million-square-foot Dallas Galleria on the market, it tossed into the package the nearby Galleria North shopping center and a 432-room Westin Hotel. The transaction was menu-driven, so buyers could choose to purchase all three properties or just one or two. In the end, UBS Realty, a division of UBS AG, Switzerland's largest bank, bought the shopping mall for $300 million. The Galleria North was eventually sold to Chicago-based RREEF, while Hines kept the Westin.[7]

DON'T FORGET THE SMALL THINGS

What it actually takes to sell a building is a whole bunch of small tasks that should be done by a broker, not necessarily by you. This doesn't mean you give up oversight of the transaction. Even if a broker is handling the sale, you still have to make sure the broker does everything necessary to make the deal happen in a timely manner, working toward a favorable outcome.

Whether you sell the property yourself or hire a broker to do the street work, have a checklist of tasks that should be performed: for-sale signage creation, flyer and brochure printing and distribution, listing the property on Internet real estate Web sites and other databases, and the preparation of various advertisements.

ENCUMBERED PROPERTIES ARE A TOUGH, BUT NOT IMPOSSIBLE, SALE

In these complex times, properties are often acquired in complex transactions. Sometimes it seems finding a cleanly owned piece of real estate is rarer than discovering a diamond in Arkansas.

Owners can often use property as collateral for issuing bonds or as the basis for mortgage financing. Olympia & York began to build its empire only after it discovered the benefits of first-mortgage bonds. These instruments are issued by the developer and backed by the triple net leases of the tenant, generally a government agency or triple-A-rated corporation.

Financial encumbrances simply have to be worked around. In 2003, AIMCO, a Denver-based multifamily REIT, put a 12-property portfolio worth $150 million on the block. Seven of the 12 complexes were cross-collateralized and sold as a package. They were backed by $57 million worth of bonds that could be assumed by the buyer.[8]

In another instance of encumbered properties, an investment group led by an affiliate of Emmes & Co. sold a portfolio of 20 multifamily apartment complexes in the Mid-Atlantic states to a New Jersey investor for $280 million. The properties were part of a 10,800-unit portfolio that once served as collateral for two defaulted bond issues. Emmes and its affiliates bought the mortgages on the portfolio in late 1997 from an investment bank.[9]

Through its great growth years, Olympia & York routinely mortgaged its assets. It would issue bonds secured by any of its office towers, such as 55 Maiden Lane in Manhattan. Despite these encumbrances, the company's major assets in Canada and the United States could have been sold in the late 1980s to raise cash. Why were they not? According to author Bianco, Reichmann took advantage of the abundant tax write-offs and deferrals that flowed from mortgage-financed property ownership. "Eventually, the tax bill would come due, but the more buildings that Olympia & York owned and the more debt it carried, the longer it could put off tax day."[10]

The strategy was part of Olympia & York's undoing. To pay for his penultimate development, Canary Wharf in London, Reichmann borrowed against the company's portfolio of trophy properties throughout North America. He even hocked his beloved First

Canadian Place office tower in Toronto, which Olympia & York developed to be the tallest building in Canada. Olympia & York's $475 million offering, which was backed by the First Canadian Place, was at the time the largest corporate bond issue in Canadian history.[11]

SOMETIMES IF YOU DON'T SELL, YOU LOSE

As World War II began to close on the family of Renee and Samuel Reichmann, they moved first from Vienna to France, then to Morocco, and finally to Canada. The family's first business venture in the New World was a company that imported tiles. At one time or another Paul and his siblings, Albert, Edward, and Louis all tried their hands at real estate. But it wasn't until Paul and Albert joined forces in 1964 that Olympia & York Industrial Development was formed as the forerunner of Olympia & York Development.

After specializing in small- to medium-size warehouses, Paul and Albert took a major step forward by buying into the Flemingdon Park development in suburban Toronto and building it out to completion. From here, Olympia & York jumped into downtown Toronto development, including the erection of First Canadian Place. In 1977, Olympia & York ventured into the United States with the purchase of a portfolio of office buildings in Manhattan. It continued to expand across the United States with other purchases and developments, including the World Financial Center, which stood in the shadow of the World Trade Center. The company then turned its attention to Europe and, in particular, London.

The modern history of Canary Wharf, perhaps Olympia & York's most storied property, begins in 1980 when the London Docklands Development Corporation (LDDC) was created by the local government to regenerate the area. Two years later, British developer

G. Ware Travelstead proposed building a 10-million-square-foot office complex on Canary Wharf. Travelstead was unable to fund the grand scheme, and it was taken over by Olympia & York. In 1987, after a light-rail line to Canary Wharf was completed, Olympia & York signed a master building agreement with LDDC for a 12.2-million-square-foot development.

As noted, 1987 was just about the time when real estate markets were beginning to fall apart in North America and London. Undismayed, Paul Reichmann held to his great vision and plowed on, with the first big topping out occurring in 1990.

As *Time* magazine reported, at one point Paul and Albert Reichmann were among the world's richest men. "Lords of a vast real estate, resource, and railroad empire that spanned Canada, the U.S., and Europe with a total value estimated at $12.8 million," is how the magazine described them. Then recession hit, real estate values plunged, and Canary Wharf quickly began hemorrhaging money. All the while, the Reichmanns mortgaged up instead of selling their real estate. By then it was too late. In 1992 Olympia & York filed for bankruptcy, as did Olympia & York Canary Wharf Ltd. (which technically went into Administration).[12]

IN REAL ESTATE THERE ARE ALWAYS SECOND ACTS

Paul Reichmann's vision of Canary Wharf as a second office market for London was brilliant. Given time and more capital it surely would have succeeded. In fact, it did eventually succeed, just not as Reichmann had originally expected. One year after filing for bankruptcy, 11 lender banks refinanced the project with an injection of $1.8 billion. Already, numerous American firms had taken up space at Canary Wharf. By the time of the recapitalization, 7,000 people were working there. That same year, the Jubilee underground line

MEET THE MAVERICKS

Paul Reichmann

Birth Date: 1930

Occupation: Cofounder, Olympia & York Development; Chairman of Canary Wharf Group PLC; Chairman of IPC US Income Commercial REIT, Toronto, Canada

Education: No degree

Career Highlights:

- Founds O&Y Development
- Develops First Canadian Place, Toronto
- Buys portfolio of eight high-rises in Manhattan, its first move into the United States
- Develops World Financial Center in Manhattan
- Builds vast Canary Wharf development

began construction out to the development, thus smoothing traffic flow to the area.

By 1994, almost 30 shops and restaurants were open. Important British firms such as the *Daily Telegraph* relocated to Canary Wharf, and there were more than 10,000 employers in the area.

Reichmann's concept was to continue to expand Canary Wharf through the various economic cycles, observes Harry Rannala, a real estate analyst with Raymond James in Toronto. "It was so large it could never be fully developed in one economic cycle," Rannala says. "What happened to Reichmann was that he ran out of equity.

But the proof of Reichmann's reasoning is in the pudding; Canary Wharf is quite successful today."

Paul Reichmann never lost sight of the project he started. In 1995 he led a consortium of investors stretching from New York to Saudi Arabia in a buyout of the property. While Reichmann ended up with only a small ownership position, he was once again in charge of the development. Four years later, Reichmann took the project public as the Canary Wharf Group. When the initial public offering's smoke had cleared, Canary Wharf boasted a market capitalization of $3.6 billion.[13]

In a typical showing of Reichmann's trademark optimism, he declared in a September 2002 company report: "The Canary Wharf estate currently has more than 14 million square feet of office space completed or under construction. We now have the potential to lift the development to around 20 million square feet and the ability to respond to client needs over the foreseeable future."[14]

In the report, Reichmann made a quick reference to "a challenging market."[15] It was a typical Reichmann understatement. In fact, Reichmann was in danger of losing his Canary Wharf a second time.

After going public in 1999, Canary Wharf rode a then-hot market to trade at a huge premium to the value of its properties. When the market turned, the development's financial services tenants were hard hit and demand evaporated. By mid-2003, vacancies jumped to the 20 percent range. On top of that, Canary Wharf shocked the market when it revealed that some leases gave tenants the option to hand back significant amounts of space for temporary periods.[16]

With the company ailing, opportunistic buyers began circling around the property, including Morgan Stanley's European Real Estate Fund and Canada's Brascan Corporation, which already owned a 9 percent stake in Canary Wharf.

This time around, Canary Wharf's management team indicated it would work with a buyer. Because the sale was still pending as this book went to press, what this meant for Paul Reichmann remained unclear. "Morgan Stanley may be the most friendly bidder toward management and is possibly preparing a joint bid that includes present management," notes Neil Downey, an analyst with RBC Capital Markets in Toronto.

Although Brascan has a history with Reichmann, it is not expected to include Paul Reichmann in its plans if it makes a play for Canary Wharf.

CREATE NEW OPERATING UNITS TO BUY YOUR OLD PROPERTIES

After the collapse of Olympia & York, the Reichmann family's real estate interests ended up in five different publicly traded companies, including Canary Wharf Group, which, as of this writing, is still under the chairmanship of Paul Reichmann.

In 2001, a Canadian company called IPC US Income Commercial REIT went public with an eye to becoming the first Canadian REIT to offer substantial exposure to the U.S. commercial real estate market. The company owns 20 office buildings/complexes and six retail centers, mostly in second-tier markets. It was founded by Paul Reichmann in 1998. In 2003, the Reichmann family retained a 23 percent interest in the REIT, plus 51 percent voting control of the company.

Perhaps indicating that the acorn really does not fall far from the tree, Paul's son, Barry Reichmann, runs one of Canada's most respected real estate companies—Retirement Residences REIT. It ranks as Canada's largest owner and operator of retirement and long-term-care facilities. In 2003, it owned and managed 180 centers in Canada and 28 facilities in the United States. The origins of Retirement Residences dates back to 1994, when Paul Reichmann, Barry

Reichmann, and another investor bought 70 percent ownership of a small retirement and nursing home chain. After astutely growing the business, it, too, went public in 2001. Barry Reichmann carries the titles of president and chief executive officer.

"Paul Reichmann sold his stake in the company earlier in 2003," notes Sam Damiani, a vice president and director with TD Newcrest in Toronto. Indeed, Barry's father sold 4.5 million REIT units to a syndicate of investment dealers, saying he wanted to focus his investments on the Canary Wharf project in London.

The most aggressive, risk-taking members of the next generation of Reichmanns to master the art of real estate investing were Philip Reichmann, Albert's son, and Frank Hauer, Paul's son-in-law. The two had been running the Olympia & York Development's property management unit. In 1993, after the bankruptcy, they bought back the property management and leasing arm, called Olympia & York Properties. Then, in a series of smart corporate moves, they created a bigger, publicly traded real estate powerhouse.

Robert Campeau, another Canadian corporate empire builder, attempted through a series of large takeovers (Allied Stores and R.H. Macy & Co.) to become a real estate and retail supermaven through his Campeau Corporation. But with $13 billion in debt, it all went bust. The Reichmanns took major losses in the blowup of Campeau Corporation (at one time they were the second-largest shareholders in the company), which by the mid-1990s was a mere shell of its former self and called Camdev Corporation, but was still listed on the Toronto Stock Exchange.

In 1997, Philip Reichmann, now chairman and chief executive officer, merged his private company into the publicly traded Camdev, creating a new entity, the publicly traded O&Y Properties Corporation. As part of the deal, they raised $50 million in O&Y Properties common equity and soon started buying portfolios of real estate. "We grew the portfolio by further acquisitions of smaller portfolios and individual properties," explains Philip Reichmann.

MEET THE MAVERICKS

Philip Reichmann

Birth Date: 1957

Occupation: Chief Executive Officer, O&Y Properties; Chief Executive of O&Y Real Estate Investment, Toronto, Canada

Education: Attended Talmudic College

Career Highlights:

- Buys out Olympia & York's Property Management Business
- Buys Camdev Corporation and merges it with O&Y Properties Inc. to form O&Y Properties Corporation.
- Buys First Canadian Place, Toronto
- Spins off O&Y REIT
- Develops Maritime Life Tower, Toronto

"In 1999, the company acquired the interest in First Canadian Place [Olympia & York Development's former flagship property] in downtown Toronto. Through the years, we really focused on the two sides of our business: one being the ownership of office buildings; the other being a very large real estate services business."[17]

Also in 1999, O&Y Properties bought Enterprise Group, a real estate service business, creating at the time Canada's largest third-party commercial property management business, operating across the country in every major market.

Both young and experienced investors often face the situation where they have accumulated a good portfolio of properties throwing off a comfortable yield, but to expand further they must increase the return from that portfolio. There are myriad ways to do this. Paul Reichmann preferred to mortgage his existing portfolio. By leveraging his properties, he is able to use the capital to create new developments.

Philip Reichmann employed a different strategy. Realizing the stock market was not properly valuing the projects O&Y Properties held, he spun out a publicly traded REIT called O&Y REIT. He then sold real estate from O&Y Properties to the new entity, which was majority owned (50.05 percent interest) by O&Y Properties. It was a good move.

"In 2001, O&Y REIT was created and a $150 million IPO was successfully launched," Philip Reichmann recalled. "O&Y REIT used the proceeds, along with the issuance of new debt and the assumption of existing mortgages, to acquire 16 office properties from O&Y Properties Corporation."[18]

What was not included in the REIT spin-off was First Canadian Place. The 72-story tower was developed by Olympia & York Development and lost in bankruptcy, but later recovered "for a ransom paid to the banks of nearly $400 million."[19]

As RBC's Downey notes, "O&Y Properties bought back the crown jewels from the old empire."

IF YOU CANNOT SELL, FIND OTHER WAYS TO UNLOAD YOUR PROPERTY

First Canadian Place boasts 2.5 million square feet and would have dominated O&Y REIT, says Raymond James's Rannala. "There are rules regarding the size of a single asset within a REIT, but more importantly there were some tax problems. The building has been depreciated over the years, so to sell it would have realized a very significant tax bill."

Philip Reichmann solved this problem by allowing O&Y REIT to own a 25 percent interest in the project through a loan. O&Y REIT received an economic interest in First Canadian Place in return for a $55 million participating loan to O&Y Properties. The loan allowed O&Y REIT to participate in the income and value growth of the building.

Like his uncle, Philip Reichmann enjoys the fruits of creative financing. He describes O&Y Properties as a company with four areas of business: an interest in O&Y REIT, a real estate services business, ownership of First Canadian Place, and a new office building development.

O&Y Properties' major development is the 441,000-square-foot Maritime Life Tower in Toronto, which was completed in March 2003. At the time of O&Y REIT's IPO, it made a mezzanine development loan of $40 million to O&Y Properties in connection with the development of the Maritime Life Tower. It has an option to purchase the buildings at development cost anytime prior to September 2004.

Sometimes, as Paul Reichmann learned, creative financing can come back to bite you. Maritime Life, the first new office tower in Toronto in a decade, opened in the heart of another deep real estate recession and was stuck at being just 50 percent leased.

The Toronto office market was very weak in 2003, probably as bad as it has been since 1995, avers Rannala, "and it will get worse." What that bodes for Maritime Life, he adds, "is that the economies of the building have not lived up to what was anticipated."

The 2002 corporate report for O&Y Properties noted that "leasing activity . . . has been slowed by the same softness experienced in most market segments across the country." But, Philip Reichmann stayed positive. "We remain optimistic that when the market does turn around, it will do so in a manner that will see our space in the Maritime Life Tower taken up quickly."[20]

SELL DOWN YOUR PROBLEMS

O&Y Properties still owns about 8.4 million square feet of space in 21 office properties, the majority of which is the 2.7-million-square-foot First Canadian Place.

Since its IPO, O&Y Properties, under its O&Y Enterprises, reduced the number of square feet it has under management to about 80 million, plus it holds a 60 percent interest in a partnership with CB Richard Ellis Facilities Management, servicing a portfolio of more than 74 million square feet.

With the onset of a new recession at the start of the millennium, O&Y Enterprises entered a difficult period. As a result, it underwent a substantial restructuring. Seeing these problems, unlike his uncle, Philip Reichmann decided to minimize the ongoing risk by selling a portion of the company's western regional portfolio of service contracts.

"The company effectively grew too quickly and ended up taking on some contracts that were basically not profitable, so it is not managing as much in terms of square footage as it did a couple of years ago," Downey said.

Rannala is even more frank: "The property arm has stumbled in the last year or so. It was anticipated by management to grow very dramatically; in fact, the reverse has happened."

The problem, says Rannala, is endemic to the business, particularly in slow times. "It's very competitive, especially in terms of margins. It takes a lot of infrastructure. When you go into a new city, you have to establish operations and personnel. It is very expensive to do all that."

Also based in Toronto, O&Y REIT owns a portfolio of 19 multitenant and government office buildings, totaling 4.7 million square feet at last count. If the complaint against O&Y Properties was that it tried to grow the service side of the business too quickly, Philip Reichmann got the formula right on the aggregation side. By being cautious, O&Y REIT now has very low debt levels.

In May 2003 Downey noted, "O&Y's debt to gross book value currently sits at 36 percent to 37 percent. This relatively small REIT [assets of $715 million] can comfortably acquire $150 million of assets, which is substantial to the existing asset base."

O&Y REIT found itself in such a strong position because it elected not to take action on some acquisition opportunities that would have exposed it to market risk. Summing up the current environment, Philip Reichmann said, "While market conditions remain unsettled with more buyers than sellers, we will stay with our proven strategy of acquisition discipline. We will not take on unnecessary risk."[21]

It was a good strategy because O&Y REIT was able to sit out when property prices were peaking. When the market turned and sellers had to sell, O&Y moved in. "They have been on a major acquisition binge in 2003," says TD Newcrest's Damiani. "The numbers are approaching $200 million in assets over the last six months."

Some of it was just catching up. For example, recent deals included acquiring the remaining 50 percent interest in two Edmonton properties for C$23.25 million. However, the company also bought a 300,000-square-foot, 19-story office building in downtown Toronto for C$72.6 million and announced it was acquiring for C$69 million a 50 percent interest in Winnipeg's TD Center.

Is Philip Reichmann as shrewd as his uncle Paul? "It's a different environment today," Damiani says. "Paul Reichmann could triple his money on an investment, but it has been difficult for anybody to do that over the last few years. Philip Reichmann has made some good plays. His one development in Toronto [Maritime Life] hasn't worked out well yet, but most of his other deals have been good. Even buying back First Canadian Place, I'm sure he's making money on that asset today."

If there is one difference between Paul Reichmann and Philip Reichmann, it is that the younger man has a greater aversion to risk. Paul Reichmann was considered to be something of a gambler. The type and scale of development deals that Philip Reichmann has done and the very conservative leverage ratios he has maintained show him to be more cautious.

Damiani adds, "The cowboy nature of real estate that existed 15 years ago doesn't exist today. Capital, from a debt and equity perspective, is far more disciplined than it was back then. Philip Reichmann has embraced this new reality wholeheartedly and has been doing a decent job along the way."

THE MAVERICK APPROACH TO SELLING TO YOUR ADVANTAGE

1. Not selling is sometimes the biggest mistake you can make.
2. You should consider selling when times and conditions are good, even if you don't have to for financial reasons.
3. Be on the lookout for signs the market has reached a peak. This is your signal to get out.
4. If you own more than one property, and conditions are ripe for selling, trim those assets that are least important to your bottom line first and ensure that the sale is in line with your overall business strategy.
5. Don't immediately decline an offer to buy your property, even if you currently have no plans to sell. It may be an offer that is too good to refuse. Alternatively, you might be able to return to that same party once you are ready to sell.
6. If you cannot get your asking price for the property, be ready to compromise.
7. Selling involves a bunch of small tasks—such as advertising and listing the property—that are best handled by a broker. Still, it's up to you to keep an eye on the broker and make sure the sale takes place on your terms.
8. Unloading property with a financial encumbrance is tough, but not impossible, if you are willing to work around it.
9. Remember, there are always second acts in real estate. If you fail to sell at the right moment the first time around, chances are you will get another opportunity to do so down the line.

Continues

10. If you are unable to sell your property to a willing buyer, look for other ways to unload it.

11. If necessary, sweeten the deal for the buyer to make the transaction go through.

Notes

Chapter 1

1. Howard Rudnitsky, "Patience Pays," *Institutional Investor Online*, 2000.
2. Donald Trump, *Trump: The Art of the Deal* (New York: Warner Books, 1993).
3. Ibid.
4. Ibid.
5. Donald Trump, *Trump: The Art of the Comeback* (New York: Times Books, 1997).
6. Ibid.
7. Ibid.
8. Ibid.
9. Ibid.
10. "New York Area's Top Privately Held Companies," *Crain's New York Business*, November 25, 2002.
11. Peter Grant & Joseph Hallinan, "Is Donald Trump Slipping Again?" WSJ.com Real Estate Journal, February 18, 2002.
12. Trump, *Trump: The Art of the Comeback.*
13. Jerome Belson, "Now Built, Trump World Tower Wins Over Critics," ABO Development, fall 2002.
14. Trump, *Trump: The Art of the Deal.*
15. Ibid.
16. Ibid.
17. Ibid.

Chapter 2

1. "Real Estate Cycles & Outlook 2002," Torto Wheaton Research, p. 6.
2. Glen Mueller, "Real Estate Market Cycle Monitor," Legg Mason Equity Research, May 2002.

3. Peter Chinloy, "Real Estate Cycles: Theory and Empirical Evidence," *Journal of Housing Research,* 1996, p. 1.
4. "New York Area's Top Privately Held Companies," *New York Crain's Business,* November 25, 2002, p. 23.
5. Donald Trump, *Trump: The Art of the Comeback* (New York: Times Books, 1997).
6. Jane Bower Zastrow, "A Big Building Buyer Hangs Tough," *Grid,* November 2001, p. 41.
7. Ibid.
8. Dana Dubbs, "Shorenstein Spread Its Wings," *Commercial Property News,* March 16, 2002, p. 1.
9. Zastrow.
10. Dubbs.
11. Dubbs.

Chapter 3

1. "Is Donald Trump Slipping Again?" WSJ.Online, February 18, 2002.
2. Sheila Muto, "What's Brewing in the Real Estate Market; East-West Venture," *Wall Street Journal,* April 16, 2002.
3. "Glossary," www.constructionwork.com.
4. "Towards Greater Transparency in Real Estate Private Equity Funds," www.upenn.edu, July 31, 2002.
5. Steve Bergsman, "Vulture Funds Present Declining Opportunities," *Barron's,* November 19, 2001.
6. Ibid.
7. Steve Bergsman, "Carving Out A New Asset Class," *Investment Dealers' Digest,* December 1, 1997.

Chapter 4

1. "Glossary of REIT Terms: Cash Flow," www.mack-cali.com.
2. Wendy Tanaka, "High-Riser," *San Francisco Examiner,* December 19, 1996.
3. Don Konipol, "Private Mortgage Loans Provide A Short-Term Financing Alternative," *Commercial Investment Real Estate,* May/June 2002.
4. Ibid.
5. Ibid.
6. "Acquisition History: August 2002," www.copt.com.
7. Steve Felix, "Smooth Sailing with Great Lake REIT," *Institutional Real Estate Letter,* June 2002.

8. "The Future for REITs," Torto Wheaton Research, March 26, 2001.

9. Peter Grant, "Office Landlords Take a Hit as Leases Begin to Expire," *Wall Street Journal,* May 22, 2002.

10. Anthony W. Deering, "Real Estate Today: The New Realities," *The Business Monthly,* July 1998.

11. Ibid.

12. Lindie Clark, *Finding a Common Interest* (New York: Cambridge University Press, 2002).

13. Ibid.

14. Ibid.

15. "Our Story, Our Future," Lend Lease 2000 Annual Report to Shareholders.

Chapter 5

1. Miriam Lupkin, "The LeFrak Legacy," *Multifamily,* April 2000.

2. Ibid.

3. Chris Barnett, "On The Pier," *Urban Land,* November/December 2001.

4. Ibid.

5. Sana Siwolop, "2 Large Cargo Buildings in Hands of a New Owner," *New York Times,* September 18, 2002.

Chapter 6

1. Donald Trump, *The Art of The Deal* (New York: Warner Books, 1987).

2. Ibid.

3. "SF Bay Area Developer's Portfolio," www.urbanecology.org.

4. Steve Bergsman, "The Self-Storage Parking Debate: When Is Enough Really Enough," *Mini-Storage Messenger,* February 2003.

5. Bill Mundy, "Defining Trophy Property," *The Appraisal Journal,* October 2002.

6. Ibid.

7. John McLoud, "Retailing Woes Continue, but Will Real Estate Hold the Course?" *National Real Estate Investor,* May 1, 1996.

8. Ibid.

9. Trump, *The Art of the Deal.*

10. Jill Margo, *Pushing The Limits* (New York: HarperCollins Publishers, 2000).

11. Clifford Pugh, "High Points," *Houston Chronicle,* July 14, 2001.

12. Daniel Fisher, "Second Empire," *Forbes,* October 30, 2000.

13. Ibid.

14. Ibid.

15. Ibid.

16. Kate Murphy, "An Appreciation for the Numbers," *New York Times,* October 8, 2000.

17. Cynthia Hoffman, "The Convert," *Architecture,* March 2002.

18. Jessica Miller, "An Expanding Empire," *National Real Estate Investor,* July 2002.

19. Murphy.

Chapter 7

1. Steve Bergsman, "Old Land; New Use," *Area Development,* August 2002.

2. Glossary, "Vulture Fund," www.investment.com.

3. Brian O'Reilly, "Sam Zell Is One of America's Biggest Landlords. So Why Isn't He Worried?" *Fortune,* October 13, 2002.

4. Terry Savage, "Terry Savage Talks Money with Sam Zell," *Chicago Sun-Times,* March 26, 2000.

5. "Strategy," www.skyharborutah.com.

6. Stephen Quazzo and Andrew Hess, "Evaluating Office Properties for Acquisition," *Development,* spring 2002.

7. "New Boston Fund Sells 200 Great Pond Office Building," www.newbostonfund .com.

8. Steve Bergsman, "From Mills to More," *Urban Land,* April 2003.

9. Anthony Bianco, *The Reichmanns* (New York: Times Books, 1997).

10. Ibid.

11. Ibid.

12. Ibid.

13. Ibid.

14. Steve Bergsman, "Carving Out a New Asset Class," *Investment Dealers' Digest,* December 1, 1997.

15. O'Reilly.

16. Peter Linneman and Stanley Ross, "Real Estate Private Equity Funds," www .theshortrun.com.

17. Ibid.

18. "The 25 Most Influential People in Real Estate," *Realtor,* December 1, 2000.

19. O'Reilly.

20. Bill Vlasic, "Pragmatic Partners," *Michigan Today,* spring 1997.

21. Ben Johnson, "BOMA 1996: When Zell Speaks, Everyone Listens," *National Real Estate Investor,* September 1, 1996.

22. Ibid.
23. Vlasic.
24. Johnson.
25. Vlasic.
26. O'Reilly.
27. O'Reilly.

Chapter 8

1. Brian O'Reilly, "The Property Master: Sam Zell Is One of America's Biggest Landlords. So Why Isn't He Worried?" *Fortune,* October 13, 2002.
2. "Equity Office to Acquire Spieker for $7.2 billion," *Institute of Real Estate News,* February 26, 2001.
3. "The Market Perspective: Equity Office Properties and Spieker Properties," Torto Wheaton Research, March 2, 2001.
4. "Bubble (W)Rap," Grubb & Ellis Co., December 2002.
5. O'Reilly.
6. "Dreamer, Builder and Teacher," *Lifestyles,* 1991.
7. TCR Organizational Structures Operating Philosophy, www.tcresidential .com.
8. Ibid.
9. Stefani C. O'Connor, "The Lefrak Organization: Welcoming the Challenges of Hotel Development," *Hotel Journal,* September 2000.
10. Ibid.
11. "Dreamer, Builder and Teacher," *Lifestyles,* 1991.
12. Peter Grant, "Lives and Times of the Century's Classic New Yorkers: Better Homes and Gardens, Sam LeFrak," *Daily News,* May 13, 1999.
13. Ibid.
14. Linda Yglesias, "Across the River and into the Wall," *Daily News Magazine,* April 29, 1990.
15. Richard Karp, "The World According to Samuel J. LeFrak," *Financial World,* April 2, 1991.
16. Ibid.
17. Linda Yglesias, "Across the River and into the Wall," *Daily News Magazine,* April 29, 1990.
18. "Dreamer, Builder and Teacher," *Lifestyles,* 1991.
19. Yglesias.

Chapter 9

1. Steven Lowy, address to PCA/AFIRE Leadership Conference, April 10, 2003.
2. Ibid.
3. "Utilize In-House Asset & Property Management," www.bedfordproperty.com.
4. Ibid.
5. Steven Lowy, address to PCA/AFIRE Leadership Conference, April 10, 2003.
6. "Standardize Forms, Procedures, and Documentation," www.faegre.com.
7. "The Power to Get It Done," www.prudentialltm.com.
8. Frank Lowy, address before Annual General Meeting of Westfield Holdings Ltd., November 12, 2002.
9. Ibid.
10. Steven Lowy, address to PCA/AFIRE Leadership Conference, April 10, 2003.
11. Ibid.
12. William Neuman, "Grand Zero Snag," *New York Post,* April 4, 2003.

Chapter 10

1. Donald Trump, *Trump: The Art of the Comeback* (New York: Times Books, 1997).
2. Robin Sidel and Dean Starkman, "Bid for Taubman Could Confront New Legal Hurdle," *Wall Street Journal,* February 24, 2003.
3. David Ambro, "Hot Debate Over Home Depot Plan," www.smithnetny.com.
4. "Business Real Estate Depreciation Deductions: Cost Segregation Analysis & Reporting," Rainmaker Marketing, www.real-estate-consultant.com.
5. Roy E. Cordato, "Destroying Real Estate Through the Tax Code," CPA Journal Online.
6. "Kaufman & Broad Inc.," www.scripophily.com.
7. Eryn Brown, "Nailing the Housing Boom," *Fortune,* September 30, 2002.
8. Ibid.
9. Dean Foust, "They Can't Build 'Em Fast Enough," *Business Week,* March 11, 2002.
10. Queena Sook Kim, "The Super Model Home; Builders Unveil Pricey Extras for Once-Uniform Houses; $250 for the Shapely Toilets," *Wall Street Journal,* August 6, 2002.
11. "CEO Interview: KB Home (KBH)," *Wall Street Transcript,* August 13, 2001.
12. Kim.
13. "CEO Interview: KB Home (KBH)," *Wall Street Transcript,* August 13, 2001.
14. Brown.

15. Brown.
16. Foust.

Chapter 11

1. Dean Starkman and Robin Sidel, "Taubman Is Dealt Setback in Battle Against Takeover," *Wall Street Journal,* May 9, 2003.
2. Dean Starkman and Robin Sidel, "Mall Brawl: Bid Marks REIT Turning Point," *Wall Street Journal,* April 28, 2003.
3. Ibid.
4. Thomas Corfman, "Rodamco Fights Hostile Bid by World Trade Center Mall Owner," *Chicago Tribune,* September 14, 2001.
5. Ibid.
6. Starkman and Ridel, "Mall Brawl."
7. Starkman and Sidel, "Mall Brawl."
8. Marcie Geffner, "Negotiating to Yes," www.realtor.com.
9. "MHC's Bid for Chateau Long Time Coming," *SNL Real Estate Securities Weekly,* May 12, 2003.
10. Starkman and Sidel, "Mall Brawl."
11. Michael Fickes, "Gimme Shelter," *Shopping Center World,* April 1, 2003.
12. Ibid.
13. Jana Madsen, "Simon Says," *Buildings,* May 2002.
14. Ibid.
15. Jana Madsen, "Best of the Best," *Buildings,* May 2002.
16. Madsen, "Simon Says."
17. John Roberts, "Simon Property Group: Recommend Purchase of Largest Mall REIT with Buy Rating," www.stifel.com.
18. Ibid.
19. Janet Morrissey, "Will a Takeover Battle Spark Merger Activity?" *Wall Street Journal,* May 16, 2003.
20. Starkman and Ridel, "Mall Brawl."
21. Morrissey, "Will a Takeover Battle Spark Merger Activity"
22. Morrissey.
23. Madsen, "Simon Says."

Chapter 12

1. Anthony Bianco, *The Reichmanns* (New York: Times Books, 1997).

2. James Frantz, "Blackstone Places Strategy On Risk/Reward Investing," *National Real Estate Investor,* June 1, 1999.

3. Ibid.

4. "Time Is Right for Sale-Leaseback Financing," *Frontiers,* spring 2001.

5. Ibid.

6. David Heaton, "Beacon Completes $279 million Sale to MIT," *National Real Estate Investor,* April 1, 2001.

7. Christine Perez, "Dallas Galleria: Bull-Headedness Wins the Deal," *Dallas Business Journal,* March 3, 2003.

8. Parke Chapman, "AIMCO to Sell 12-Property Apartment Portfolio," *National Real Estate Investor,* March 12, 2003.

9. "Emmes Group Sells Portfolio," www.propertynews.com.

10. Anthony Bianco, *The Reichmanns.*

11. Anthony Bianco, *The Reichmanns.*

12. Michael Serrill, "To Catch a Canary," *Time,* September 4, 1995.

13. Thomas K. Grose, "Singing a Different Tune," *Time,* April 5, 1999.

14. "CEO Provides a Brief Historical Sketch and an Overview of O&Y Properties," *Wall Street Transcript,* February 11, 2002.

15. Ibid.

16. "Morgan Stanley Seeks Canary Wharf," *Wall Street Journal,* June 9, 2003.

17. "CEO Provides a Brief Historical Sketch and an Overview of O&Y Properties."

18. "CEO Provides a Brief Historical Sketch and an Overview of O&Y Properties."

19. Albert Warson, "Back From Oblivion—With a Bang," *Building,* November/December 2002.

20. "A Disciplined Approach," Annual Report 2002 O&Y Properties Corporation.

21. Ibid.

Index